C000180358

WALKING WITH WELSH LEGENDS
NORTHERN WALES

By the same author:

Walking with Welsh Legends: South-west Wales

Walking
with Welsh Legends
Northern Wales

Graham Watkins

First published in 2012

© Graham Watkins

© Llygad Gwalch 2012

All rights reserved. No part of this publication
may be reproduced, stored in a retrieval system,
or transmitted in any form or by any means, electronic,
electrostatic, magnetic tape, mechanical, photocopying,
recording, or otherwise, without prior permission
of the authors of the works herein.

ISBN: 978-1-84524-176-6

Cover design: Lynwen Jones

Published by Llygad Gwalch,
Ysgubor Plas, Llwyndyrys,
Pwllheli, Gwynedd, Wales LL53 6NG.

www.carreg-gwalch.com

*Dedicated to
my walking companions
Tricia and Honey,
who have shared
the pleasure of these walks
with me.*

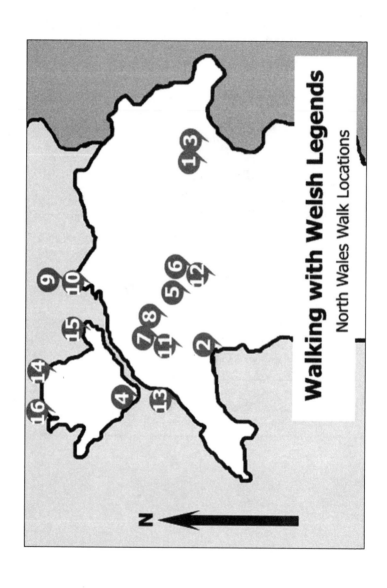

Walking with Welsh Legends

North Wales Walk Locations

Contents

Introduction

Wales is a land filled with legends. Every breathtaking valley, towering mountain and shimmering lake has its own tale to tell. This book will help you discover secluded rivers, castles and golden beaches, all with stories to entertain and enchant. The culture of Wales and its history are interwoven with legends that cross the centuries. The very land itself adds to the mysticism, with its variety and beauty.

Here, for your enjoyment, are sixteen Welsh legends that have been retold and linked to the land where the stories took place. This is the second book in the series and deals with popular legends from north Wales. Each legend is accompanied with details of a walk that you can do to explore the story further and enjoy the scenery in which the events you have read about took place.

Climb Mount Snowdon and look down on Bwlch y Saethau (*bwlch*: pass; *saethau*: arrows), where King Arthur fell, mortally wounded, in his last battle. Explore the magical island of Llanddwyn, where Princess Dwynwen, the patron saint of lovers, made her home. Visit Gelert's grave and learn how the faithful hound died at his master's hand. These are just three examples of the stories and walks within these pages.

Many pieces of Welsh folklore are repeated and there are variations of the same story relating to different places. At the same time, some places are associated with several legends. To avoid confusion and repetition, where legends are similar, I have used the story I liked best and omitted the rest. No offence is intended to partisan interests. One advantage I found of rewriting the more ancient legends is the licence to embroider. That is what storytellers have done for centuries. Nothing changes and I admit that I had a lot of fun adding my own interpretation to some of the tales.

The legends I have included are a diverse mixture. There are love stories, tales of heroic deeds, foolishness, greed, fables and humour. The cast includes fair maidens, wicked tyrants, explorers, kings, and ordinary folk quietly going about their business.

The walks are equally diverse and include mountains, sandy beaches, castles, woodland, hidden lakes and ancient towns. As I completed each walk, I found that I had a different perspective on, and a better insight into, the related legend. The walk and legend reinforced each other and added to the enjoyment. Most of the walks are not difficult and are suitable for a family to attempt together. To derive the most enjoyment, I suggest that you read the legend first and look at the map to help understand the geography of the story, before you start the walk. By doing so you will be able to pick out the relevant landmarks as you go.

The starting point for each walk can be located using the latitude and longitude coordinates given, or the map references quoted from Ordnance Survey 1:50,000 Landranger Maps. I make no claims regarding rights of way but have walked all of the routes without any problems. Equipment I would recommend includes a compass, an Ordnance Survey map, suitable footwear and appropriate clothing. The weather can change quickly, particularly on higher ground, so dress accordingly and, if it is hot, sun-cream, hats and drinking water for everyone are essential.

For those who may be interested, I have Anquet software to plot the waypoints on a computer and download them to a Garmin Etrex Venture HC to do each walk. My wife bought the GPS for my birthday after we got lost on one of the walks. As a consequence, these are toys that I have learned to use whilst researching Welsh legends and walks. They have added another dimension to the planning and I would now not go walking without them. Apart from the fact that it is a lot harder to get lost, I find the information they give me both invaluable and entertaining. One Anquet function I particularly like allows you to fly over the route, viewing it using pictures from Google Earth. Great fun! Many of the walks are well signposted, but some of the more remote ones are not and it is easy to get lost.

A word about walking speed is appropriate. I read somewhere that the British Army used to march 3 miles (4.83 km) in 50 minutes and then rest for 10 minutes before marching the next 3 miles. The speed I have quoted is rather slower at 2 miles (3.2 km) per hour with an hour added for each 300 m of climb. This is the same speed that the Welsh drovers used to walk, when driving stock across the country. It will seem slow for some, but what is the point of a pleasant walk if you don't have time to admire the views or smell the flowers on the way?

I should also take this opportunity to apologise to my wife for getting her lost more than once, and thank Dave Simkins FCCA, Graham Watkins (my cousin) and Cheryl Matthews for their constructive comments on this book, which helped immensely. While the position of features is right at the time of writing this guide, the position of stiles and gates may change from time to time and new fences and stiles sometimes get added, confusing the unwary. Many of the walks include working farmland and I would urge everyone to observe the normal courtesies of closing gates behind you if they are shut when you reach them, taking home your litter and keeping dogs under control. If you do, we will all continue to enjoy the beauty and splendour of Wales and her legends.

Graham Watkins
Garnlwyd
2012

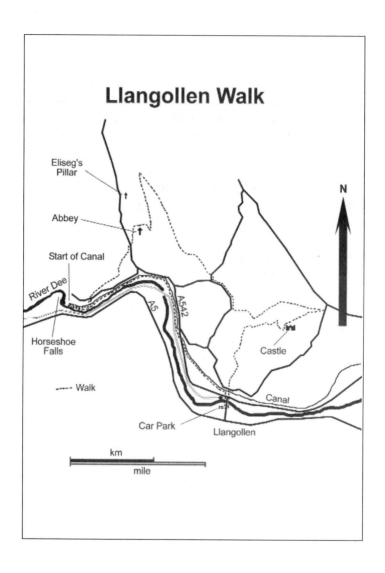

Llangollen Walk

Eliseg's Pillar

Abbey

Start of Canal

River Dee

Horseshoe Falls

A5

A542

N

Castle

Canal

Car Park

Llangollen

----- Walk

km

mile

12

1

Myfanwy the Beautiful

High above the little town of Llangollen, on the top of a great mountain, sits Castell Dinas Brân, named after the legendary Bendigeidfran (*Brân the Blessed*) from the Mabinogi. Local lore has it that his spirit lives on as ravens (*brân*: raven) that lurk amid its towering battlements; Brân is also connected to the 'White Tower' and the raven legend of the Tower of London. In the thirteenth century an earl and his family lived at Castell Dinas Brân. The earl was a wealthy man and owned much of Powys. He had a daughter named Myfanwy and he loved her very much. Myfanwy was spoiled as a child. Her father showered her with gifts of every kind. He surprised her with fine dresses of silk and damask. He had succulent foods bought to the castle for her and gave her servants orders to carry out her every wish.

Myfanwy quickly learned how to get her own way. A sly tear, a scowl, or a scream would strike fear into the hearts of her servants; they knew the power of her wrath and the strength of her sulks. The years passed and Myfanwy grew into womanhood. As she grew she changed from a pretty girl into a woman of beauty. Her long black hair and dark piercing eyes enchanted all who saw her.

News of her great beauty spread and suitors travelled from across the land to woo her, eager to win her hand and, some said, to inherit her father's wealth. A brave knight climbed the mountain to the castle and sang in praise of her loveliness, but she sneered at his songs and chatted loudly while he sang. Crushed by her rudeness, the knight retreated down the mountain.

A famous scholar journeyed to Castell Dinas Brân and recited a fine poem flattering her beauty. Myfanwy scoffed at his sonnet and walked out of the castle hall while the bard was still speaking. The frustrated poet left the castle and returned to the town below. Others tried to win Myfanwy but all were treated with the same contempt. No flattery of song or verse could satisfy the vain Myfanwy. She knew she was more beautiful than any man could describe in tune or rhyme.

Disappointed suitors filled the alehouses of Llangollen, exchanging tales of woe and drowning their sorrows. They sang to each other mournfully of Myfanwy's beauty and her conceited vanity.

Hywel ab Einion was a dreamer of a man. Night after night he listened to the songs and the poems. He had never seen Myfanwy. but the descriptions of her beauty thrilled him. He fell in love with her long black hair, her dark piercing eyes and her soft white cheeks. His romantic mind searched for a way to win her for himself – but how? For Hywel was a penniless youth. Would the beautiful daughter of an earl ever look on him as an equal, worthy of marriage?

The years passed and Hywel grew tall and strong. His upright frame and easy smile made him popular with the girls, but there was only one vision that filled his heart: the dream that he had never seen – Myfanwy.

Myfanwy had never married and still lived in the castle high above the town. No man had flattered her enough to win her heart. Each evening, after work, Hywel would look up at the castle, longing for a glimpse of Myfanwy.

One summer night as he watched the mountain and the castle he heard the sound of sweet music coming from the river. He went down to the water and found an old man playing a lute and singing. The melody danced and toyed with the noise of the tumbling water. The song entranced Hywel, as it teased and thrilled, with sensations that aroused his emotions.

Dinas Brân castle

The old man stopped playing and placed the lute on the ground.

'Old man, will you teach me how to play the lute and sing?' asked Hywel.

The old man looked at Hywel. 'Why do you want to play and sing like an old man?' asked the old man.

'Old man, your music has no age. It speaks of love and happiness, of bravery and beauty. These things are timeless. I see now that with such music I can win my love', replied Hywel.

'You speak of love, which is good. I will teach you to play the lute and sing, but the song you use to win your love must be your own,' said the old man.

They agreed, and each evening the two men would sit by the river. The old man was a good teacher and Hywel an eager pupil. He quickly mastered the lute, and as he sang, his voice grew strong and confident.

Each day while he worked, his mind was busy. He thought of the beauty of Myfanwy, of his love for her and hers for him. The words in his mind formed into couplets and verses. The song grew longer and his heart filled with pleasure.

'You are ready,' said the old man, one evening. 'Is your song ready?'

Hywel picked up the lute and began to play. He sang softly at first and then louder as his emotions took hold. Towards the end of the song, his voice grew quiet, as if his love was close by his side.

He stopped and looked at the old man, wanting his approval. Tears of joy ran down the old man's face.

'You are ready. Go now, tonight, and win Myfanwy', he said, pointing at the castle.

Hywel took his lute and climbed the mountain. The castle gate was open. There was a feast in the great hall: Sir Ralph, a knight from a distant land, was visiting. Hywel entered the hall and saw Myfanwy for the first time. His heart filled with joy. She was more beautiful than he had imagined.

He strode nervously across the hall and stood before the high table. The earl looked down at him and saw the lute.

'Come, play a merry tune for us,' he commanded.

The guests ignored Hywel and continued to laugh and talk.

Hywel lifted his lute and began to sing, quietly at first, and then more loudly as his courage grew. The crowd fell silent as he sang. He looked at Myfanwy. Her dark clear eyes returned his gaze without blinking. He sang of her beauty and she smiled. He praised her pale cheeks and she blushed. His words fell like caresses on her long black hair and she laughed, but still her dark clear eyes returned his steady gaze.

Hywel's song ended quietly, like a conspiracy between two lovers. Myfanwy stood and applauded and the guests cheered. Hywel bowed and advanced towards Myfanwy. She offered her hand and he kissed it, confident that he had won her heart. Hywel was invited by the earl to sit at the top table, and the feasting continued late into the night.

Next morning Hywel returned to the castle but Myfanwy had gone.

'Where is Myfanwy?' asked Hywel.

The earl looked at the impudent serf before him.

'She is promised in marriage to another far more noble than you,' replied the earl.

'But she loves me,' said Hywel.

'You're a fool. Myfanwy enjoyed your adulation but will never marry a peasant like you. She has gone with Sir Ralph. The marriage contract was signed yesterday,' said the earl.

Hywel stumbled down the mountain broken-hearted. According to the legend, he wrote one last poem for Myfanwy and never spoke of her again.

The real author of the famous love poem 'Myfanwy', was the Welsh poet Richard Davies. It was set to music by Joseph Parry, and published in 1875. The song is a favourite with Welsh male voice choirs. It ends with 'farewell':

> *Myfanwy, boed yr holl o'th fywyd*
> *Dan heulwen ddisglair canol dydd.*
> *A boed i rosyn gwridog ienctid*
> *I ddawnsio ganmlwydd ar dy rudd.*
> *Anghofia'r oll o'th addewidion*
> *A wnest i rywun, 'ngeneth ddel,*
> *A rho dy law, Myfanwy dirion*
> *I ddim ond dweud y gair 'Ffarwél'.*

> (Myfanwy, may you spend your lifetime
> Beneath the midday sunshine's glow,
> And on your cheeks O may the roses
> Dance for a hundred years or so.
> Forget now all the words of promise
> You made to one who loved you well,
> Give me your hand, my sweet Myfanwy,
> But one last time, to say 'farewell'.)

Ruins of Valle Crucis abbey

Llangollen canal

Llangollen Walk

The ancient town of Llangollen is the starting point for this walk. Steeped in history, and a major transport link through the years, Llangollen is intersected by the river Dee (*Afon Dyfrdwy*), the A5 (the original turnpike road built by Thomas Telford), the Llangollen Canal, and the railway, which in turn bankrupted the canal company. To the east of the town is the Froncysyllte Viaduct, where the canal crosses 120 feet above the river. Dinas Bran castle sits high above the town and our walk begins with a climb to explore the crumbling ruin. From the castle the walk continues east before turning back through a stunning valley north of the castle, where it joins the Clwydian Way taking you to the ruin of Valle Crucis abbey (*Abaty Glyn-y-groes*). From there the walk continues over Velvet Hill to Horseshoe Falls where Telford built a giant weir to divert the Dee into the canal, and finally a leisurely

Ordnance Survey map numbers 116 and 117
grid reference SJ 213 420
Latitude = 52.9703, Longitude = -3.1721
Lat = 52 degrees, 58.2 minutes North
Long = 3 degrees, 10.3 minutes West

Length	11.18 km – 6.94 miles
Maximum height	312.76 m
Minimum height	80.00 m
Height ascended	434.51 m
Navigation	Easy
Difficulty	Moderate
Estimated time	4 hours 33 minutes
Difficulty	Moderate
Estimated time	3 hours 47 minutes

stroll along the towpath back to Llangollen. The town is on the A5 10 miles south-west of Wrexham and 10 miles north-west of Oswestry. Llangollen boasts numerous hotels, public houses and restaurants. The Chain Bridge Hotel, by Horseshoe Falls, is a useful rest stop where you can relax by the canal before the last leg of the walk. There is a long-stay car park on the corner of East Street and Parade Street. This is where the walk begins.

Leave the car park and walk along Parade Street to the end, where you turn left into Castle Street and walk over the bridge, built in 1345, which crosses the Dee. This is the first stone bridge over the river and is one of the 'seven wonders of Wales'. Turn right in front of the Bridge End Hotel and then immediately left along Wharf Hill, which takes you behind the Bridge End Hotel and over the canal.

At the end of Wharf Hill, cross the road and continue straight on to steps leading to the footpath signposted 'To Offa's Dyke Path'. The footpath takes you north past a school on your left to a stile, where you continue straight on following the right-hand side of a field to a kissing gate. Go through the kissing gate and along the lane to a junction, where you continue straight on following the 'Castell Dinas Bran' sign. When you come to the next kissing gate go through it and turn right, leaving the main path.

You are now on the footpath that will take you up to the castle. Initially the path climbs to a small plateau and then descends across a small dip before zig-zagging up to the castle. As you explore the ruins you will, depending on the weather, have superb views of Ruabon Mountain (*Mynydd Rhiwabon*) to the north, the Berwyn mountain range in the south and the Vale of Llangollen to the east. A section of the 'Offa's Dyke Walk' runs along the foot of the Ruabon Mountain and when you descend you may see intrepid walkers progressing along the 177-mile route.

Leave the castle walking east along the path that starts on the right of the large wall on the east side of the ruin. The path quickly becomes a grassy slope leading down to a stile. From here it zig-zags down the hill into a field where you continue downhill, aiming for a clump of gorse bushes. The footpath goes through the gorse bushes to a gate leading to a lane. Do not go through the gate. Instead turn hard left, almost back on yourself, and walk west down the valley. There is no signpost showing the route you need to take, but after a short distance you will see a pathway following a line of stunted trees. After 500 m you will reach a stile where you continue straight on with the castle above you on your left and farmland on your right.

The footpath now turns so that you are walking south-west for another 370 m. When you reach a T-junction, turn right over a stile into the field. The footpath follows the right-hand side of the field and brings you to a stile on the far side below Dinbren Hall, the large house you can see in the distance.

When you reach the stile, cross over it into the lane and turn right. Initially the lane climbs, taking you north, and slowly turns left as you walk past Dinbren Hall. After 450 m you will reach a junction where you turn right following the signpost to 'Worlds End'. You are now on Dinbren Road. Walk 70 m along the road and turn left following the footpath sign 'Llangollen History Trail'. The track you are now on climbs north-west for 250 m where it passes behind a house and you reach a stile. Beyond the stile is a grassy footpath, which you follow. You are now on the 'Clwydian Way'.

To the south-west, in the distance, you will see a series of bridges where a road crosses the Dee and the canal. Above the road bridge is a railway bridge. Just beyond the bridges is Horseshoe Falls, the start of the Llangollen Canal, and a point you will visit later in the walk. The next 1.5 km of the walk are north-west along the Clwydian Way as it slowly descends through mature woodland into a fertile valley.

As you progress, the ruin of Valle Crucis abbey will come into view in the valley. Shortly before the abbey's dissolution in 1537 the abbot, Robert Salbri, was arrested at the abbey on charges of highway robbery and counterfeiting and removed to the Tower of London. In 1896 a Reverend Owen did some excavating in the ruin and discovered a copy of the Koran hidden in one of the walls, which he believed had been bought back from the crusades by one of the knights.

Just north of the abbey ruin, near the road, you will also see what appears to be a standing stone. This is Eliseg's Pillar (*Piler Eliseg*), also known as Guinevere's Cross. The cross was erected in the eighth century and the inscriptions on it are said to relate to King Arthur and his family.

As you reach the bottom of the valley there is a sharp left turn, which you take so that you are walking south. After a short distance the path turns right over a stile and towards a house. There is another stile just before the house, which takes you into a field on the left where you continue following the fence line on the right. Ignore the first footpath on the right and continue straight on following the signpost to 'Valle Crucis Abbey'. This will bring you to a stile leading to a track. Cross the stile and follow the track for 30 m to a gate on the right, leading down to the river and a footbridge.

Cross the footbridge and walk straight on, through the caravan park, to the entrance where you turn left along the lane. Just on your left is the abbey ruin, which is open to the public if you want to explore it. Walk 50 m along the lane and go through the metal kissing gate on the right leading into a field. From the stile, walk south across the field for 100 m to the next stile, in the far corner. This will bring you to a road where you turn left and continue south for a short distance, until you reach a footpath on the right. Walk up the footpath and cross the stile signposted as 'National Trust – Velvet Hill'. Continue uphill a short distance to a T-junction, where you turn left so that you are again walking south. Follow the path for 500 m as it meanders through the wood, bringing you to a stile and then a small road junction.

Cross the road and walk down the lane following the 'Corwen' sign. You will soon pass a picnic area on the right and reach a small gap in the wall on your left leading to some steps. Walk down the steps and over the footbridge that crosses the canal. At the bottom of the steps you will arrive at the towpath and the entrance to the Chain Bridge Hotel.

Turn right so that you are walking west and follow the towpath for 250 m until you reach Horseshoe Falls. The falls are, in fact, a weir built by Thomas Telford to divert 12 million gallons of water a day from the Dee into the canal. One consequence of this was that the downstream river level dropped and watermills, which relied on the river, became unworkable.

Retrace your steps from the falls and continue along the towpath for 2.8 km back to Llangollen. There is plenty to see during this leisurely part of the walk, including the railway sheds of the Llangollen Heritage Railway, where old rolling stock and engines are marshalled. There is also a small motor museum, and in the town itself is the arena used for the International Music Festival each July.

Shortly after you pass the narrow boat marina, you will reach a small crane on the quay and the Wharf Tea Rooms. Leave the towpath at the next bridge and return, down the hill, around the Bridge End Hotel and back to the car park.

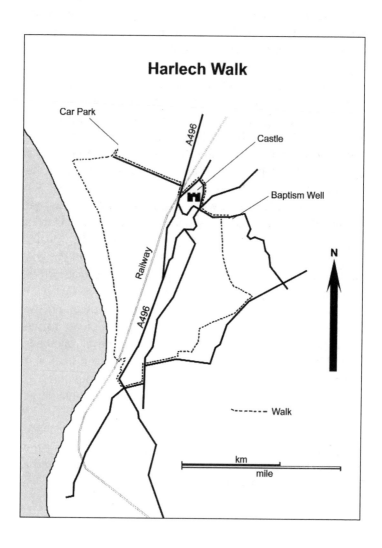

Harlech Walk

Car Park

A496

Castle

Baptism Well

Railway

A496

N

------- Walk

km

mile

2

The Men of Harlech

March ye men of Harlech bold,
Unfurl your banners in the field,
Be brave as were your sires of old
And like them never yield!
What tho' every hill and dale
Echoes now with war's alarms,
Celtic hearts can never quail,
When Cambria calls to arms.

1860 English lyrics by W. H. Baker

King Edward I built Harlech castle as part of his ring of castles designed to subdue the Welsh. The concentric design and its location, which enabled it to be re-supplied from the sea, made Harlech a formidable stronghold.

In 1404, Owain Glyndŵr starved the English garrison until only twenty-one men were left, and they surrendered. Glyndŵr then used Harlech as his base for the next four years until the English set out to recapture the castle. It took them eight months and a thousand men to retake the fortress. Glyndŵr's efforts to liberate Wales were crushed. He vanished, and the English continued to occupy Wales.

Most of north Wales, Gloucestershire and Cheshire became part of the Duchy of Lancaster, and Welsh fighting men were recruited as Lancastrian soldiers. When Edward IV came to the throne of England on 4 March 1461 the civil wars known as the Wars of the Roses had been an on-and-off affair for several years. The war between the Lancastrian and Yorkist sides of the Plantagenet dynasty was a running fight for the English throne.

Edward was a Yorkist, but there was another claim for the English throne. The Lancastrian, Henry Tudor, 2nd Earl of Richmond, was just four years old. Young Henry, a Welshman born in Pembroke (*Penfro*) from an illegitimate line, had a weak claim to the crown, but Edward could not ignore the young pretender. Henry and his supporters fled the country in fear for their lives.

They travelled to Harlech castle, where the constable, a Welshman named Dafydd ap Ieuan, helped the party escape to Scotland. Henry Tudor then went on to France, where he lived and grew to manhood under the protection of the French king.

With Henry gone from Wales, Edward quickly overran the country, confiscating Lancastrian property and executing his enemies. Harlech was besieged but refused to surrender to the Yorkist army. The garrison continued to hold out and was re-supplied from the sea, using the fortified stairway that reached 61 m (200 ft) down from the castle to the water. The castle continued to resist whilst the war raged across the kingdom. In 1465 the garrison was reinforced when the Lancastrian Sir Richard Tunstall arrived with fresh soldiers. They held out for another three years until 1468 when, thinking that the Lancastrians had lost, they finally surrendered the castle. The siege had lasted seven years. It was the longest siege in British history and Harlech was the last Lancastrian stronghold to capitulate.

Henry Tudor returned to the British Isles, landing in Pembrokeshire in 1485. He gathered an army of 5000 men and marched east to attack the Yorkist king, Richard III, at Bosworth Field. Richard was killed and Henry crowned himself Henry VII on the battlefield.

According to Shakespeare's play *Henry III* Part 1, describing the start of the 'Wars of the Roses', the two sides of the war met in Temple Church, London where they chose red and white roses for their emblems. But the scene depicted in the play has no historical basis. When the Lancastrians, led by Henry Tudor, fought at Bosworth in 1485, they fought under a Red Dragon standard, while the Yorkist's flag depicted a White Boar.

Only later did the rose emblems gain significance, when Henry came to the throne. He married Princess Elizabeth of York to cement his position as King Henry VII and end the war. Henry then combined the red rose of Lancashire with the white rose of Yorkshire, thus creating a red and white 'Tudor' rose to demonstrate the unity of his kingdom.

Henry Tudor was an able administrator who went on to establish a peaceful and stable society, which grew prosperous during his reign. The dynasty he started included Henry VIII and Queen Elizabeth I, both of whom became powerful monarchs.

Harlech castle and the courage of its garrison, withholding a siege for seven long years, are celebrated in the stirring marching song 'Men of Harlech'. It has been the regimental tune for several Welsh Regiments and has been adopted by Canadian and Australian forces. There are a number of versions of the lyrics, including one especially written for the 1964 film *Zulu*. The battle at Rourke's Drift, South Africa, depicted in the film, was an action that took place in 1879 when 139 soldiers of the 24th Regiment of Foot, later renamed the South Wales Borderers, fought off an estimated 4000 Zulu warriors. Eleven Victoria Crosses were awarded, the highest number ever presented for a single action.

Visit Harlech today and you will see the Red Dragon still flying high and proud above the ramparts of the stronghold that is Harlech castle.

The Red Dragon still flies high above Harlech castle

Men of Harlech, stop your dreaming
Can't you see their spearpoints gleaming
See their warrior pennants streaming
To this battlefield ...

As sung in the 1964 film Zulu

Harlech Walk

This is a walk starting in the sand dunes below Harlech castle, which is a Welsh Heritage Site. It takes you up and around the castle then climbs high above the town of Harlech, giving you fine views of the Snowdonia mountain ranges (*Eryri*), Llŷn peninsula, and the golden beaches of Tremadog Bay. Part of the walk, above the town, is poorly marked and there is some climbing, particularly near the beginning. The last section of the walk takes you on a leisurely 2 km stroll along the beach and back to the car park. Harlech is located on the A496 ten miles north of Barmouth (*Abermo*). There are toilets in the car park, which is pay and display. Byelaws ban dogs from parts of the beach at certain times of the year.

Ordnance Survey map number 124 grid reference SH 573 316
Latitude = 52.8635, Longitude = -4.1193
Lat = 52 degrees, 51.8 minutes North
Long = 4 degrees, 7.2 minutes West

Length	7.46 km – 4.63 miles
Maximum height	198.63 m
Minimum height	0 m
Height ascended	263.64 m
Navigation	Moderate
Difficulty	Moderate
Estimated time	3 hours 10 minutes

Leave the car park and walk east along the road towards the castle. After 700 m you reach a T-junction where you turn right along the main road. Continue along the road for 100 m until you cross the railway line. The sea once covered the flat land you are on, and the castle was at the water's edge. This made it possible to bring in supplies of food, weapons and fresh soldiers by sea when the castle was under siege. The sea has now retreated, replaced by a vast area of sand. Immediately after the railway crossing turn sharp left along Hwylfa'r Nant. There is a sign for Woodlands Caravan Park pointing in the direction you need to go. On the right you will see a stairway leading up to the castle. This was used to bring supplies up from the ships into the castle and the town, which was also fortified. Records from 1286, made during the castle's construction, show that the workforce included 546 labourers, 115 quarrymen, 30 blacksmiths, 22 joiners and 227 stonemasons. The castle cost £8,160 to build (£90 million in today's money).

Walk north-east along Hwylfa'r Nant for 300 m, passing the railway station on your left then turn right along a lane named Ffordd Pen Llech, opposite Tan-y-Castell industrial units. Walk south-east along the lane, passing the entrance to the caravan park. The lane then climbs steeply, weaving as it takes you up and around the east side of the castle, which is on your right. At the top of the lane there is a road intersection in the centre of Harlech, where you cross the junction and proceed east along Pen Dref, passing the Lion Hotel on your right.

Continue uphill along the road for 250 m, ignoring the first footpath sign on your right and leaving the road through a metal gate at the second footpath sign on the right. Before you do so, you might want to make a small detour and walk a few steps further along the road to look at a strange rectangular hole that has been formed on the right. It is a baptism well built in 1841 by 'Scotch Baptists' living in Harlech. Retrace your steps back from the well to the footpath, which takes you south for 350 m and then bends slightly to the east for another 300 m. You now walk south-east through fields with dry stone walls, which you cross using small stone steps set in the walls that act as stiles. This part of the walk is poorly signposted.

At the top of the last field, climb the stile and continue south-east towards a marker post with a yellow ring. Walk past the post to a stone stile leading to the next field. Cross the field and go over the wooden stile leading into a lane, where you turn right and walk south-west. This is the highest point of the walk and the views from here are spectacular in all directions. After 250 m you reach a ladder stile and footpath sign, leaving the lane to the right. Cross the stile and continue walking south-west across the field, aiming for the stone walls in the far corner where there is another stone stile set in the wall. The field is overgrown with gorse and bracken and, once again, the path is not clear.

Cross the stile and continue walking south-west, keeping close to the wall on your left. Go through the gap at the bottom of the field and go straight on, with the next stone wall now on your right. The village ahead of you in the distance is Llandanwg, which has an interesting medieval church near its beach. Beyond Llandanwg is Ynys Fochras (*Shell Island*), known for its seashells and wild flowers. The island was created when the Afon Artro was diverted in 1819. The island boasts a campsite where you can enjoy 'wild camping'. After 150 m you reach a gap on the wall, which you ignore. Walk on, keeping the wall on your right until you reach a stile leading to a patch of scrubland. Continue on the path as it turns west along the back of a row of houses and then turns left over a stile and through a narrow path to emerge in a lane. Turn right and follow the lane as it descends west for 300 m.

At the end of the lane you reach a road junction where you turn left, and continue downhill for another 170 m until you arrive at a crossroads. Turn right here, following the sign for the A496. After 200 m, when you reach the main road, turn right along the main road for 70 m until you reach a metal kissing gate on the far side of the road. From here you have one of the best views of the beach that stretches north for 6 km towards the Glaslyn Estuary and Portmeirion. The beach and the sand dunes, some of which are 10 m tall, are a National Nature Reserve and a Site of Special Scientific Interest.

Go through the kissing gate and follow the footpath as it zigzags down the cliff, crosses the railway line and down some steps onto the beach. Turn right along the beach and walk north for 2 km until you reach a red-and-white-striped post, where you turn right and follow the path, leaving the beach across the sand dunes. After 300 m this path will bring you back to the car park.

Harlech beach stretches into the distance

The view looking north across the Glaslyn estury towards Portmeirion

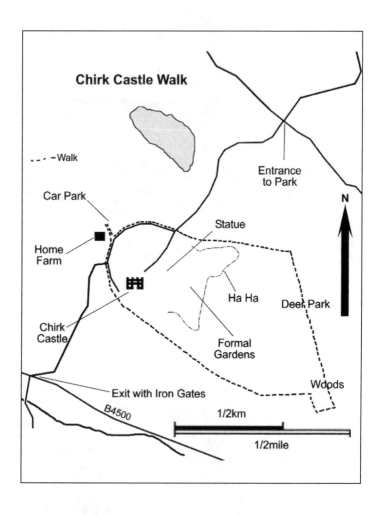

Chirk Castle Walk

- - - Walk

Car Park

Home Farm

Chirk Castle

Exit with Iron Gates

B4500

Entrance to Park

N

Statue

Ha Ha

Deer Park

Formal Gardens

Woods

1/2km

1/2mile

3

The Red Hand of Chirk

Lord Myddleton was a proud man when he learned that his beautiful young wife was with child. He had married late and needed to sire an heir to inherit his castle and estate before his ardour declined into old age. Lord Myddleton was a popular baron and the news of his wife's confinement was greeted with celebration in the towns and villages of the Marcher lands. His castle at Chirk was a happy place, with noble visitors arriving each day to offer their congratulations to the old man and his pregnant wife.

The weeks passed and the baroness started to show. Her belly grew quickly and her anxious husband, for this was his first child, summoned the doctors. They prodded and pushed the young baroness and consulted at length.

'My lord. There is nothing to fear. Your wife has healthy lungs and a strong heart. She will bear your sons and be a fine mother,' they reported.

'My sons?' cried the baron.

'Aye, my lord,' replied the doctors. 'Your wife is with twins.'

The baron was overjoyed with the news. But, he wondered, would they both be sons? If there were two sons which one would inherit his estate? The baron asked his friends for advice.

'Don't worry,' they said. 'One is sure to be a girl, then you can marry her off.'

The baron started to worry. He needed to be sure.

'Perhaps the midwife can advise you,' suggested a squire.

'Fetch her at once,' commanded the baron.

The midwife was a common woman, stout in frame and calm in nature. She listened quietly while the baron explained his problem.

'If there are two sons how will I know which should inherit my lands and title?' asked the baron. 'They cannot both be baron of Chirk.'

The midwife considered his lordship's question carefully before she replied.

'My lord, have no fear. The answer to your problem is plain enough. Is it not true that the first-born son should inherit?' asked the woman.

'That is so,' replied the baron.

'Then, when the time comes I will tie a ribbon to the first baby that emerges to identify your first-born child,' said the midwife.

The baron liked the midwife's simple suggestion and agreed to her plan.

The baroness continued to grow bigger as the months went by, until at last the time arrived for the birth. A room was prepared and the baroness withdrew. The midwife issued instructions to the women of the castle. The fires were built up to keep the birthing room hot. Boiling water was fetched, and soft linen to wrap the babies in. The baron and his squires waited for news in the great hall.

The contractions quickened. Slowly the top of a head began to emerge and then a tiny arm appeared. The midwife swiftly tied on a red ribbon. Her hands were slippery with blood.

'Push now, with all your might,' cried the Midwife.

The baroness screamed and pushed. Then she stopped, tired and wanting it to end.

'Baroness, you have a son,' yelled the midwife and held the

baby up by its legs. The child spluttered and began to cry. Its lungs were hearty. Hearing the sound, the baron ran to his wife's chambers.

'Keep out, my lord. Our work is not yet done,' called the midwife.

'Do I have a son?' demanded the baron, through the closed door.

'Aye, you do, my lord,' replied the midwife returning to her work.

She saw a tiny leg and a head appearing. The second baby was delivered. It, too, was a boy. The little body was covered in blood and on its arm was the tiny red ribbon – but because of the blood, the midwife did not see the ribbon as she wrapped the second child in its linen shawl.

The baron could contain himself no longer. He burst into the room.

'Well. Is it done?' he cried.

'It is, my lord. You have two fine sons,' replied the midwife. She handed him the little bundles.

'Which is first born?' asked the baron as he gazed at the babies.

'The one with the red ribbon on his arm,' replied the midwife, content with her reply.

As the boys grew, no one, not even their mother, could tell them apart. They were identical in size and feature. To tell the difference the baroness sewed ribbons into the sleeves of one of her son's clothes. It was he that was to become the next baron of Chirk.

The years passed and the old baron grew frail and weak. His sons grew strong and fit, competing in everything they did. They became clever and ambitious men, but one was more ruthless than the other. As the old baron's health failed he took to his bed. Feeling his life slipping away he sent for his sons.

He turned to the eldest. 'You are first-born and my rightful heir. When I am dead you will be baron of Chirk,' he said.

'How can this be so father? For we are twins,' said the second son.

'The ribbon on your brother's sleeve shows he was born before you. There cannot be two barons. You must leave and make your own way in the world,' said the baron, feebly.

The first son was pleased but his brother grew angry. This was unfair. Why should his brother get everything while he has to slink away with nothing but the clothes on his back? Slowly a plan took

Chirk castle

shape in his head. The next morning the second son woke early, dressed in his brother's clothes and went to his father's rooms. The old baron was dozing as his son entered.

'My lord, I must speak with you,' said the son, rousing his father. The baron stirred.

'We cannot send my brother away with nothing. He is your blood. You must change your will to provide for him,' said the son.

The baron smiled at his son. 'I cannot change the will. It is the law. You are the first son. The title and my wealth will pass to you,' whispered the baron.

'Very well father,' said the son. 'I will obey your dying wish.'

At that moment the other son burst into the room. 'Why are you dressed in my clothes?' he demanded.

'They are my clothes. Look, here is my ribbon,' replied the son that had woken the baron.

'Usurper. You have stolen my clothes,' cried the other.

The argument grew loud and the baron's servant came, drawn by the raised voices. They separated the sons and held them. The baron lay back weary. He looked at his sons through misty eyes, dilated with death. He knew he was passing away. His time had come.

'You must decide, my lord. Which of us is your true heir?' shouted one of the sons.

The baron beckoned his squire to come closer.

'Carry my bed to the gardens,' he whispered.

The squire ordered the servants to lift the baron's bed and take it to the garden. They propped the dying man up with pillows.

The sons stood by their father's bed.

'My sons, truly I do not know which of you is my heir, but there can only be one. I cannot decide so you will race around the castle. The first to return and touch my bed will be the next baron,' said the old man softly.

Without a word, the sons ran from the baron to the corner of the castle. One was just ahead as they turned the corner, but his brother tripped him and he fell. The second son ran on, but his brother recovered and chased after him. They pushed and shoved as they ran, both determined to win the fateful race. As they entered the garden one brother pushed the other into a yew tree. The fallen son, seeing that the race was lost, snatched a sword from a nearby guard and with a mighty blow cut off his own hand. He seized the bloody hand and threw it towards the baron's bed where it landed and won him the race.

From that day the coat of arms of the Barons of Chirk has included a bloody red hand.

Chirk Castle Walk

The Chirk castle walk is the shortest and easiest walk in this book, taking you around the castle and exploring the eighteenth-century parkland. The castle was built in 1295 by Roger Mortimer to guard the *Ceirog* valley and was purchased by the Myddleton family in 1595 for £5000. The Myddleton family continued to live there until 2004. The National Trust now owns the castle. The staterooms and formal gardens, which are not part of our walk, are worth visiting. There is a charge for visiting the gardens and the castle. Chirk (*Y Waun*) is 6 miles north of Oswestry (*Croesoswallt*) on the A5, 7 miles east of Llangollen and 9 miles south of Wrexham (*Wrecsam*). The castle is well signposted but it is worth checking opening times before your visit. There are toilets and a shop next to the car park.

Ordnance Survey map number 126 grid reference SJ 267 383
Latitude = 52.9375, Longitude = -3.0917
Lat = 52 degrees, 56.3 minutes North
Long = 3 degrees, 5.5 minutes West

Length	3.11 km – 1.93 miles
Maximum height	195.05 m
Minimum height	156.64 m
Height ascended	63.13 m
Navigation	Easy
Difficulty	Easy
Estimated time	1 hour 10 minutes

From the car park, walk south past the information office and follow the road uphill towards the castle. Just before you reach the castle there is a small footpath leaving to the right, signposted by a post with a red ring. Red-ringed posts are positioned along

41

much of the walk. Follow the footpath away from the road so that you are walking south through woodland with a high stone wall on your left.

After 300 m the path bears left so that you are walking southeast, and as you continue you pass a bird-watching hide on your right. The path continues for 340 m until it splits and you go right, continuing downhill for another 60 m. The Ordnance Survey map describes this wood as 'Deer Park', so if you keep quiet you may be lucky enough to see some.

The footpath now reaches a mud track where you turn left and continue for 140 m to a wooden gate. Go straight on through the gate. The path now emerges from the wood and after a short distance, if you turn and look back to your left, you will see the clipped hedges of yew that are part of the formal gardens. Continue straight ahead until you reach the next wooden gate, where you go straight on for 150 m to where the track turns right, then 70 m further on you reach a gate leaving the track on the left.

The gate takes you into Deershed Wood. Go through the gate and walk east for 100 m to a T-junction in the path where you turn left. Walk north for 400 m to a gate leading from the wood into open parkland interspersed with mature trees. Continue north across the park following the red way-markers, with the castle and formal gardens on your left.

The statue that you can see silhouetted against the skyline is of Hercules. It was commissioned by Robert Myddleton in the 1720s and placed by the entrance to the castle, but removed and dumped in the woods in June 1750, only to be rediscovered and rescued by an RAF helicopter in 1983. There is a Latin inscription on the base recording the statue's rescue and flight from the wood.

After 320 m the footpath reaches a kissing gate where you turn left, following the fence-line west for 80 m to another kissing gate, where you continue straight on. The path climbs gently

Manicured yews in Chirk castle gardens

towards the formal gardens on your left, which are protected by a 'ha-ha', where the ground falls away to a wall, the idea being that the deer cannot enter the gardens but at the same time the views from the gardens are uninterrupted by the barrier.

The path now travels north-west to a gate leading onto the road leading to the castle. Follow the sign for the car park and walk west along the road. This will give you good views of the front of the castle and, after 350 m, will bring you back to the car park and the end of the walk.

As you drive out of the castle estate it is worth stopping and looking at the huge wrought iron gates that have been erected on the drive. They were ordered by Robert Myddleton in 1711 and were built by Robert and John Davies, blacksmiths of Croesfoel Forge near Wrexham. It was agreed that the men would be paid 2 shillings (10p) a day for their labour. The finished gates are dated 1719 and the 'bloody red hand of Chirk' is in the top centre.

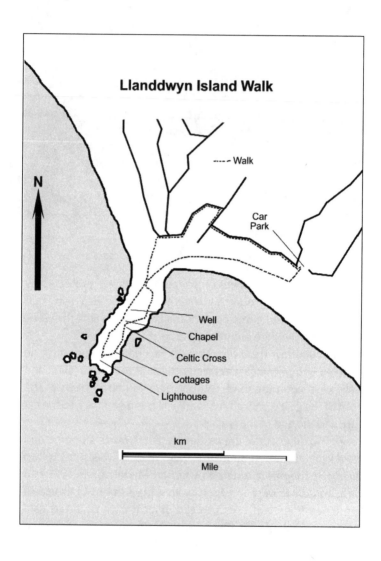

Llanddwyn Island Walk

- - - - Walk

Car Park

Well

Chapel

Celtic Cross

Cottages

Lighthouse

N

km

Mile

4

Dwynwen the Blessed

Dwynwen deigr ariendegwch ...

(Dwynwen, whose beauty is [like] hoarfrost tears ...)

*From a thirteenth-century poem by Dafydd ap Gwilym,
translated by Gwyn Thomas*

Dwynwen was a princess, one of twenty-four children sired by King Brychan Brycheiniog in the fifth century. She lived on the island of Anglesey and was loved and cherished as a child. Dwynwen grew to be a beautiful and clever young woman.

Her father, King Brychan, enjoyed the good things of life and his palace was a merry place where dancing and feasting often continued far into the night. Many young men would visit the court of King Brychan eager to win the hand of the beautiful princess. Dwynwen would flirt and tease her suitors with gay chatter. She would listen to their proud boasts of bravery and dance with them until her legs ached. But when the feasting and dancing were over, she would quickly lose interest in each new admirer.

One day a messenger arrived at the castle. 'The King of Gwynedd is to visit you, my lord. It is a great honour,' said the messenger.

'And so it is,' replied the king. 'Tell your master we shall have a royal banquet to celebrate his coming to my kingdom,' he added.

Plans were made for the great day when the two kings would feast together. The finest cattle were slaughtered, poultry plucked and suckling pigs prepared for roasting. Sweet fruits were gathered and fine cheeses matured. Brychan commanded that his best wines were fetched from the cellars. Beer was brewed and the great hall made ready. Tables were laden until they groaned with the weight of the fine delicacies.

The king of Gwynedd and his entourage were greeted with pomp and ceremony. The banquet began. The king of Gwynedd had his son with him: Prince Maelon, who some called Maelon Dafodrill. Maelon saw Dwynwen and admired her beauty. He heard her gay laughter and at once resolved that he would marry her.

The princess was quickly aware of his interest and toyed with his emotions. At first she pretended to ignore his advances. Then, she encouraged him with broad smiles and direct gazes into his eyes. Maelon became a lovesick puppy as she teased him. They danced together and, seizing the moment, he spoke.

He whispered as he held her, 'Dwynwen, my princess. I worship and love you like a goddess and I can feel your love burning for me. Shall I speak with your father? Tell me you will be mine,'

Dwynwen stiffened in his arms. 'Do not tease me, Maelon. We cannot marry. You have only known me for a few hours. Let us enjoy the evening and have no talk of love or marriage,' she replied.

Maelon refused to accept her answer and the following day he visited Brychan.

'King Brychan, I wish to marry your daughter. We are in love and I ask you for her hand,' he said.

'But does she love you?' enquired Brychan.

'I am sure of it, my lord. I saw the love in her eyes as we danced last night,' replied Maelon.

Dwynwen was summoned and the question put to her.

'Do you love Prince Maelon?' asked her father.

'I do not,' answered the defiant princess.

'There is your answer. Tomorrow you shall return to your own kingdom,' said Brychan to Maelon.

Bewildered and angry, Maelon withdrew, but that night, his last chance to see Dwynwen, he visited her in her chambers. True to her nature, she began to tease him once more, unaware of the dangerous passion she was arousing . . .

The next morning the king of Gwynedd, with his followers and Maelon, left for home.

The young princess felt ashamed and confused. She dare not tell her father what Maelon had done – it would mean war. Dwynwen left the palace and wandered into the forest. She found a sunny glade with a small river where she lay down and cried herself to sleep.

As she slept she dreamed that an angel appeared and asked why she was sad. In her dream, she replied that she hated Maelon and wanted him dead. She cried again as she told the angel what the prince had done. It was almost dark when she woke.

There was a great commotion when Dwynwen returned to the palace. News had come from Gwynedd: Maelon had turned into a block of ice. Dwynwen hurried to her chamber. Her heart was broken, for now she knew she loved the prince.

That night the angel from her dream returned.

'I beg you to release Maelon from his ice prison,' she cried.

'I cannot release your prince but I grant you three wishes. Use them well,' replied the angel.

'Release Maelon and let him live a good and honest life,' whispered the princes.

'What are your other wishes?' asked the angel.

'I pray that God will watch over and protect all true lovers. And my last wish is that, in penance for my vanity, I may never marry,' said Dwynwen.

You have chosen your wishes well,' said the angel, and vanished.

Maelon thawed completely, recovered from the ordeal and went on to live a good life. He married and raised a family.

Dwynwen left the palace and moved to a small island, where she built a chapel. She placed a golden statue in the chapel, kept lit with a hundred candles day and night. People travelled to the shrine in pilgrimage to ask Dwynwen to pray for their souls.

Nearby was a well where a strange eel lived. Women would come to ask Dwynwen if they had found true love. To answer their question, she sent them to the well where they threw bread on the water and covered it with their lover's handkerchief. If the surface remained smooth the love was true, but when the love was false and the man a cheat, the eel would devour the bread in a flurry of anger.

Dwynwen never married. When she died in 465 AD she was buried beneath the chapel she had built. She had paid for her vanity and lived a blessed life. She became the Welsh patron saint of lovers and her feast day is 25 January.

The chapel and the well are now in ruins but Llanddwyn, the island named after her, is still the perfect place to visit with your true love.

Llanddwyn Island Walk

The walk at Llanddwyn starts in the sand dunes and takes you along the 'Blue Flag' beach of Llanddwyn Bay to the island. You then explore the island including the ruined chapel and lighthouse before returning to the car park through Newborough (*Niwbwrch*) forest. The beach and pathways are all easy to follow and very little climbing is involved. Access to the Island is across the beach and Llanddwyn can be cut off during some high tides so it is best to check tide times beforehand. Views of Snowdonia, Llŷn peninsula and Caernarfon Bay are spectacular. Llanddwyn Island is in the south-western corner of Anglesey (*Ynys Môn*), 11 miles from the Menai Bridge. Take the A4080 and follow the signs for Newborough Forest and Llanddwyn beach. To reach the car park you need to use a short toll road through the forest (take some pound coins for the machine), but the toll cost includes parking fees. There are toilets at the car park. The beach is a popular destination for families keen to enjoy the golden sands and the views.

Ordnance Survey map number 114 grid reference SH 405 634
Latitude = 53.1440, Longitude = -4.3854
Lat = 53 degrees, 8.6 minutes North
Long = 4 degrees, 23.1 minutes West

Length	6.12 km – 3.80 miles
Maximum height	33.40 m
Minimum height	0 m
Height ascended	98.05 m
Navigation	Easy
Difficulty	Easy
Estimated time	2 hours 13 minutes

Leave the car park and walk over the dunes to the beach and turn right, so that Llanddwyn island is ahead of you and the mountains of Snowdonia are at your back. Walk 1.35 km along the beach, following it as it turns slowly left towards the island and brings you to a small slate roof structure with a sign welcoming you to Llanddwyn, 'the Lover's Island'. The sign tells a different, sanitised, version of the legend: one where Dwynwen merely rebuffs her suitor's advances. I prefer the version related here.

Go past the sign and turn left, following a small path up some steps. After 250 m you reach a wooden gate where the path climbs, following the line of a fence on your right. Look out for wooden posts inscribed 'Ynys Llanddwyn', which mark the path. You now walk along the east side of the island, discovering hidden beaches and rocky islands where cormorants dry their wings in the sun and seals can often be seen frolicking in the water.

About 200 m after the gate there is a bench seat, ideal for a coffee break, with one of the best views of Caernarfon Bay and Snowdonia. Continue on along the path for another 70 m until the path turns right, where a small lighthouse, two stone crosses and the chapel ruins come into view. The path now proceeds along some stone steps to the first cross. This is a Celtic cross bearing the inscription:

They lie around did living tread.
Whose sacred ground now silent dead.

A short distance west of the cross is the ruin of Dwynwen's chapel where, it is said, she was buried. From the cross, walk south along the wider path, towards the cottages. Pilots, waiting for vessels wanting to navigate the Menai Strait, used the cottages and one has been refitted with period furniture. There is a small exhibition in the cottages, which is free to visit. The island was also home to a lifeboat station here until 1903, when it was closed.

The ruin of St Dwynwen's chapel

Llanddwyn island as you approach it,
with the cross and the lighthouse visible in the distance

Celtic memorial cross on Llanddwyn island

Leave the cottages and walk south towards the larger lighthouse, which was used until the 1970s and marked the entrance to the Menai Straits. In 2004 it was used as a set for the film *Half Light*, starring Demi Moore, when the lighthouse was painted red and a fake light was added to the top using computer graphics. The real lamp was actually at the base of the tower and the opening can be seen on the far side of the lighthouse as you walk around it.

Walk back down the steps from the lighthouse and continue straight on following the white path, made from crushed seashells, that climbs up to the left of the modern-looking cross. This is the monument to Princess Dwynwen and bears the inscription:

In memory of St Dwynwen,
Jan 25 – 465

From the memorial, walk north rejoining the main path that takes you back past the ruined chapel. Shortly after the chapel you pass the freshwater well, used to divine true love, although little remains of the well today. Continue on over the cattle grid, making your way off the island.

When you reach the welcome sign you passed earlier, continue walking north so that you leave the island on the left side of the causeway. As you leave the island the large rocks should be on your right. Walk towards the sand dunes ahead of you and pass through the first gap, then make your way over the dunes to a forestry track where you turn right.

You are now entering Newborough Forest, renowned for its populations of red squirrels and ravens. Walk east for 100 m to a junction where you turn right and continue east for another 100 m. The track now turns north-east for 400 m before turning east once more. After 180 m turn right at the T-junction so that you are walking south-west towards the sea. Continue in this direction for 200 m until you arrive at a metal barrier across the track where you turn left.

You now walk south-east through the pine forest for 1 km, until you arrive back at the car park.

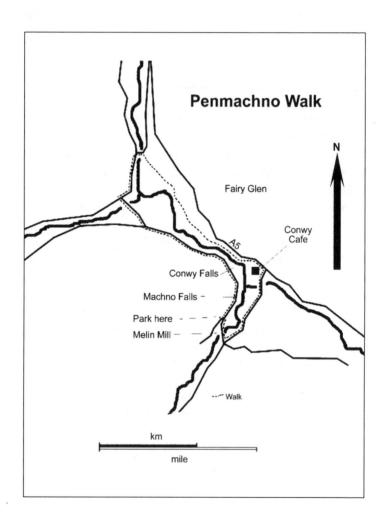

Penmachno Walk

N

Fairy Glen

Conwy
Cafe

A5

Conwy Falls

Machno Falls

Park here

Melin Mill

Walk

km

mile

5

The Gwiber of Penmachno

One day a visitor came to Penmachno and called on Rhys Ddewain. 'Tell me about the Gwiber,' said Owain ap Gruffydd.

Rhys Ddewain was an old man. He studied his inquisitive caller, wondering why this brash young man was interested in the Gwiber.

'It's a foul evil beast. Have nothing to do with it,' replied the old man.

'Tell me more of this evil beast,' demanded Owain.

'The Gwiber is a giant snake with wings. Its body is covered in slime and stinks of putrid death. It slithers on the land, can fly through the air, and lurks in the river where it feeds on fish and unwary animals that stray near the water,' said the old man.

'Such a beast must be killed and that is what I have come to do,' said Owain ap Gruffydd and drew his sword. The blade glinted in the sunlight.

'You are brave but foolish. Many have tried to rid us of the Gwiber but all have perished. Put up your sword and go home. You are no match for the Gwiber,' said the old man.

'Old man, you are weak and afraid, but I am not. I will kill this snake,' said Owain.

'You are right. I am afraid of the Gwiber and rightly so. If you hunt the Gwiber, I tell you now, it will kill you,' said the old man.

'If you can see my future, old man, tell me, how will I die?' demanded Owain.

'The Gwiber will bite your neck,' replied the old man.

That night, as Owain tried to sleep he considered what Rhys Ddewain had foretold. If it was true he would indeed be foolish to hunt the Gwiber. As he tossed and turned he resolved to test the truth of the old man's prophecy. The following morning Owain dressed as a vagrant and, so disguised, called once more on Rhys Ddewain.

'They tell me, old man, that you can see the future,' said Owain.

'That is true,' replied the old man.

'Then pray tell me, when my time comes, how will I die?' asked Owain.

'Your death will be violent, painful and very soon. You will slip while you are out walking and the fall will break your neck,' replied Rhys Ddewain.

The following day Owain put on a miller's apron, covered his face with flour and returned to the old man's house for a third time.

'Good morning, Master Miller. What can I do for you?' asked the old man.

'Can you tell me the nature of my death?' asked Owain.

'Master Miller, I am sorry to tell you that your time is short and when your end comes it will be by drowning,' replied the old man.

Owain threw off the miller's apron and wiped the flour from his face. 'Rhys Ddewain, your prophecies are false,' cried Owain. 'You have predicted three different deaths for me'.

'You will see. Time will tell,' was all the old man would say.

Convinced that the old man was lying, Owain at once resolved to find and kill the Gwiber. He collected his armour and sword and set off along the riverbank below the village. As he went he prodded the water and slashed the bushes with his sword.

'Come forward, Gwiber, and meet your end,' he yelled.

A rush of wind tore along the valley and caught Owain by

surprise. It was the Gwiber. The great serpent grappled with Owain, its wings flapping furiously. Owain tried to lift his sword but the beast trapped his arm with its coils. A foul stench began to overwhelm Owain. He felt faint. His strength was slipping away as the snake began to crush him. Suddenly the Gwiber bit deep into Owain's neck and blood ran down his chest. The beast gave a great roar and released Owain. Owain slipped on the slimy ground and fell. His head hit a large rock. There was a loud crack as his neck snapped. Owain's body continued downward into the river where he took his last breath and drowned.

The people of Penmachno found his body floating in the water later that day and carried it back to the old man's house.

'What should we do?' they cried.

'You must kill the Gwiber,' replied the old man.

The men collected their bows and spears and set out to find the great snake. They searched the valley until they found the serpent sleeping by the river. A volley of arrows and spears woke the Gwiber, inflicting many wounds. The Gwiber rose up and tried to fly, but its wings were torn and twisted. The animal writhed on the ground snarling and spitting at its attackers.

A second flight of arrows hit the beast and it howled in agony. Suddenly, the Gwiber slithered towards the villagers and, arrows spent, they backed away. They watched, with horror, as the evil snake gave one last roar and slid into the river, where it vanished forever.

Look closely as you walk along the riverbank at Penmachno, for some say that the Gwiber's eyes can still be seen looking up from the deepest pools. The place is now called Wibernant, and in the Welsh language a *gwiber* is a viper or an adder.

Penmachno Walk

Thundering waterfalls, ancient roadways, woodland and a Fairy Glen are all here to enjoy. This is a walk that is easy to navigate and most of the route is along quiet lanes. The Penmachno walk is located south of Betws-y-coed. Follow the A5 for two miles from the town and turn right along the B4006 signposted to Penmachno. Go along the B4006 for half a mile and turn right down a small lane opposite the Ebenezer chapel. Drive over the river bridge and continue on for a short distance to a small turning on the left where there is a parking area. There are toilets at the Conwy Falls Café.

Ordnance Survey map number 115 and 116 grid reference SH 806 528
Latitude = 53.0615, Longitude = -3.7822
Lat = 53 degrees, 3.7 minutes North
Long = 3 degrees, 46.9 minutes West

Length	5.43 km – 3.37 miles
Maximum height	146.89 m
Minimum height	23.47 m
Height ascended	237.39 m
Navigation	Easy
Difficulty	Moderate
Estimated time	2 hours 28 minutes

Leave your car and walk south along the lane you arrived by. When you get to the river bridge you will see, on your left, a delightful ancient stone arch over the Afon Machno. This is an old packhorse bridge, believed to have been built during Roman times, and was superseded by the bridge you are standing on. The Penmachno Woollen Mill is on the right of the road. The mill was powered by the Machno and turned local wool into woven

The packhorse bridge over Machno river

products. Richie Thomas, a famous Welsh tenor, worked at the mill from 1921 to 1971. The mill continued to operate as a mill and retail outlet until the 1990s, when modern Health and Safety regulations forced it to close. One feature of the mill, used to draw the attention of passing tourists, was a long-drop toilet, high above the river, where a dummy was left sitting in full view of the road.

Continue on past the mill for 100 m to a road junction, where you turn left and walk along the B4006. Follow the road for 900 m, passing over a river bridge that crosses a deep gorge high above the Conwy. When you reach the A5, turn left past the Conwy Falls Café. If you are interested in having a closer look at the Rhaeadr Graig Llwyd (*Conwy Falls*), there is a turnstile beside the café, leading down to the river.

The Conwy Falls Café was originally a wooden hut but in 1938

The Conwy thundering through the gorge

Sir Clough Williams-Ellis, famous for building Portmeirion, the Italian-style village near Porthmadog, drew a design for a new café. Although his design was not used, the resulting building is quite unusual.

From the café you continue along the A5 for 140 m, when the footpath leaves to the left, down some steps and takes you north-west. The path now descends downhill through woodland with the river far below you on your left. After 100 m you reach a wooden gate, which you go through and continue straight on.

About 400 m further on there is a ladder stile and gate, where the path continues north-west following a stone wall on your left.

After 300 m you come to another ladder stile where the path emerges from the wood and widens into a track with stone walls on both sides. The width of the track, at 8 m, and the quality of the stone walls suggests that at some time in the past this track was a main road. Continue along the track for 250 m to the next ladder stile, where the track narrows as it continues to descend into the valley. After 100 m you pass a tiny stone building, now locked and shuttered. Was this an early tollhouse?

Continue along the track until you pass a stone chimney and barbecue area on your left. This is Fairy Glen (*Ffos Noddyn*), a privately owned part of the valley, which you can pay to visit. The entrance is a little further along the track on the left, opposite Cwmanog Isaf Farm. Payment for visiting the Fairy Glen is made using an honesty box. Walk on past the entrance to Fairy Glen until you reach the road with the Fairy Glen Hotel on your right. Turn left along the road and cross the river bridge so that you are walking west.

Once you have crossed the river, go over the road and turn left along the slate-chipping footpath next to the cliff. After 200 m you pass a plaque on your right proudly declaring that the road and footpath were improved in 2005. Assembly Member Andrew Davies unveiled the plaque on 13 January and, no doubt, the dignitaries all retired to the Fairy Glen Hotel to celebrate the occasion. From the plaque, the path continues south and you pass a derelict eighteenth-century tollhouse, another reminder of road improvements. It was the tollhouses from this period that led to the Rebecca Riots (see *Walking with Welsh Legends: South-western Wales*, the first book in this series).

Continue along the path for another 180 m until you reach Ivy Glen House on your right. Cross the main road and take the lane opposite the house so that you are walking south-east. The lane takes you over the river and begins to climb. After 350 m you reach a junction with a signpost on your right advertising Tŷ Mawr Wybrnant tearooms, operated by the National Trust. Wybrnant can suggest 'valley of the Gwiber' and is a reference to the legend. Tŷ Mawr Wybrnant was the birthplace of Bishop William Morgan, the first man to translate the complete Bible into Welsh. After graduating from Cambridge he spent seven years studying the Bible texts in Greek, Hebrew and Aramaic. His translation was published in 1588. The house has been restored to its sixteenth-century appearance.

Go past the sign for Tŷ Mawr Wybrnant and follow the lane east, passing three cottages on your right. There is a pull-in for cars 250 m on the right beyond the cottages, and a narrow opening through the hedge on the left, which is easy to miss. Leave the lane and go through the hedge and follow the path for a short distance; it will take you down to the river, with stunning views as the water thunders through the gorge below.

Retrace your steps back to the lane and continue on, passing Conwy Falls as you walk. After 800 m you arrive at a good vantage point looking upstream along the Conwy as it tumbles down the valley. Some people call this view 'The Grand Canyon'. Far below you in the valley, hidden from view, Afon Machno joins the Conwy.

From here, the lane turns south for 200 m and brings you to the Machno Falls, another spectacular sight. The derelict building you see near the waterfall was once a corn mill but the waterwheel has long since gone. Continue along the lane as it turns south-west and after 270 m you will arrive back at your car.

The footpath follows an ancient track

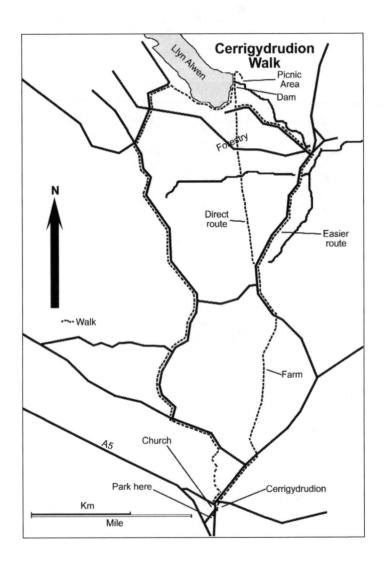

Cerrigydrudion Walk

Llyn Alwen

Picnic Area

Dam

Forestry

Direct route

Easier route

Walk

Farm

Church

Park here

Cerrigydrudion

A5

Km

Mile

6

The Demon of Cerrigydrudion

'Do you see it, over there in the window, a face?' asked the farmer quietly.

The innkeeper peered at the church and then he saw it: a hideous face staring out through the dirty glass. The eyes were sunken and cold, the cheeks white with the pallor of death itself.

'What is it?' whispered the innkeeper as the two men backed away from the apparition staring out from the little church.

News spread quickly through the village of Cerrigydrudion and a small crowd gathered in the road outside the church. The priest arrived.

'What's going on?' he asked.

'There in the window, Father! It's the Devil himself!' cried the villagers.

'The Devil! Superstitious nonsense. There's no devil in my church: It's a house of God,' cried the priest and marched along the path to the door of the church. The face in the window watched him approach. The priest took hold of his cross, held it up and opened the door.

The crowd watched as the priest disappeared into the church. They looked back at the window. The face had vanished. There was a muffled scream and the priest stumbled backwards out of the church. He turned and staggered through the churchyard, his face contorted with fear.

'What happened, Father?' cried the crowd.

'It's Satan. He is here,' sobbed the priest and started to shake violently.

The crowd looked back at the church. The evil face stared back at them from the window.

Days passed. Each day the evil face would stare out from the church. Each night strange screams and manic laughter were heard coming from the church. A dog that wandered into the churchyard vanished. The people grew afraid and would not go near the church, not even to worship on the Sabbath.

In desperation, the villagers sought out a wise man for advice. 'What can we do?' asked the farmer.

'You will need great charm to tempt the Devil from the church and great strength to drag him away,' replied the wise man.

'You must find a beautiful girl to tempt him and you must use great strength to remove him from your village,' said the wise man.

'We are not strong enough to move the Devil,' wailed the people.

'Go to the mountain and catch the Dau Ychain Banawg,' said the wise man.

The villagers knew of the two huge oxen called Dau Ychen Bannog that grazed on Waen Bannog. They listened carefully as the wise man told them what needed to be done.

A beautiful young girl called Eira Wyn (snow white) was chosen to tempt the Devil. She was dressed in silk and the women brushed her long golden hair until it shone. Men searched the mountain and found the great oxen. They tempted the beasts to return to the village with sacks of corn. The blacksmith forged stout chains and soaked the links in holy water. An enormous sledge was built using tree trunks for runners. While the villagers worked, the Devil sneered as he peered through the window of the church.

When all was ready, Eira's seven brothers bought her to the church. The Devil watched as the girl entered the churchyard. He smiled at seeing such a pretty offering. The face disappeared from the window and the door swung open – but the girl did not go into the church. Instead, she started to arrange flowers on the graves and began to sing.

The girl's innocent beauty and her sweet voice excited the Devil. Attracted by the girl and with wicked thoughts in his mind, the Devil swaggered from the church into the daylight. The villagers were ready. They rushed into the churchyard. The Devil roared with laughter as they grappled with him.

'You puny people cannot hold me,' he cried, but he was wrong.

The people flung the stout chains soaked in holy water around the Devil and pulled them tight. Still the Devil roared with laughter. The Dau Ychen Bannog were yoked to the chains. The powerful beasts dragged the Devil from the churchyard. He lay in the road kicking and screaming.

'I will have my revenge on you,' he cried.

The Devil was chained to the sledge made of tree trunks and more chains were tied to the evil demon, to make sure he was held fast. The women greased the tree trunks with pig fat to help the sledge move. Slowly, the huge beasts began to drag the Devil away. The oxen strained every sinew as the evil load shuddered and jolted along the track. The people pulled the chains and pushed the sledge to help it on its way, while the Devil cursed and shouted foul insults with every step.

After hours of toil the Devil and his captors reached a lake on Hiraethog mountain but they did not stop. The Dau Ychen Bannog, and the sledge with its evil load, kept on going and marched slowly into the water. They were never seen again. The people named the lake Llyn y Ddau Ychen (*the lake of the two oxen*) in honour of the brave beasts that perished that day.

Today, the lake is part of Alwen Reservoir, but if you look closely at the track you can still see the ruts cut by the sledge that took the Devil to his watery resting place.

Cerrigydrudion Walk

This walk starts near the church in the village of Cerrigydrudion, which is located on the A5 fifteen miles east of Betws-y-coed and seventeen miles west of Llangollen. The walk goes north across open farmland towards the Alwen Reservoir. As you climb away from the village the views are outstanding and quite different from other walks in north Wales. I have marked the walk as hard to navigate and difficult to walk for two reasons: the second half of the outbound walk to the reservoir involves crossing boggy ground, which will be difficult in winter; and as you get closer to the reservoir, the footpath goes through Forestry Commission land where the path has not been maintained and trees have been allowed to block the way. The path here is passable, but involves navigating through the wood using a compass or GPS and scrambling across tree trunks or under fallen branches. An alternative, easier, route to the reservoir is available using a quiet road, which I have shown on the map. There are tables and

Ordnance Survey map number 116 grid reference SH 952 486
Latitude = 53.0252, Longitude = -3.5621
Lat = 53 degrees, 1.5 minutes North
Long = 3 degrees, 33.7 minutes West

Length	11.54 km – 7.17 miles
Maximum height	405.98 m
Minimum height	270.30 m
Height ascended	310.79 m
Navigation	Hard
Difficulty	Hard
Estimated time	4 hours 40 minutes

Cerrigydrudion church

benches near the dam, which are ideal for a picnic. The return walk to the village is along forestry tracks and little-used country lanes, and once again you will enjoy spectacular views. Cerrigydrudion is the highest point on the A5 between London and Holyhead (*Caergybi*). There are parking spaces and public toilets on Ffordd Tan Lan, a road just south-east of the church.

Walk north from your car to St Mary Magdalen church. There has been a church on the site from 440 AD and it would have been from here that the Demon was dragged away. Across the road from the church there is a plaque above the door of what was once the Almshouse, a home for six destitute members of the parish. It was Robert Price, a local man who became a senior judge and Member of Parliament, who endowed the Almshouse. Queen Anne made him Baron of the Exchequer in 1702.

From the church, walk north past the White Lion public house on your left. Prime Minister David Lloyd George was once trapped here by a heavy fall of snow and forced to stay the night. Queen Victoria is also known to have stayed in the village on her way to Ireland. Just after the White Lion, bear left along the B4501 signposted Llyn Brenig. Continue out of the village and along the road for 750 m until you pass two houses on the left. Just past the second house is a ladder stile on the left, which you cross. You then go over a small bridge and walk north-east across a field for 150 m until you reach a hedge, where you turn right keeping the

Looking back towards the village

hedge on your left. After 300 m there is a metal gate. Go through the gate and continue straight on for 80 m to a second gate, where you continue, aiming for farm buildings ahead of you. Go through the next gate and walk towards the left-hand side of the large buildings, where there is another metal gate taking you through a dry-stone wall and into a large field.

The footpath here follows the stone wall on the right-hand side of the field and leads to a ladder stile in the top right-hand corner. Cross the ladder stile into the next field and continue north, aiming, once again, for the top right-hand corner of the field where there is a metal gate. When we last did this walk (August 2009), the farmer kindly warned us that there was a bull in the field. The bull was docile enough but very large. Fortunately, since my wife is not a fast runner, the beast was occupied with his harem and we proceeded to cross the field unmolested. Section 59 of the Wildlife and Countryside Act, 1981 prohibits certain breeds of bulls from fields that contain footpaths, but we did not stop to ask his pedigree. Leave the field through the metal gate and walk straight ahead for 70 m to a stile leading to a road where you turn left.

Walk along the road for 560 m, ignoring a lane on your left, until you reach a gate and a footpath sign leaving the road to the left. You now have a choice. If you are prepared to negotiate the boggy ground and navigate your way through the wood, leave the road following the footpath sign.

If you prefer the easier walk avoiding these obstacles, keep going along the road. The easier route continues along the road for another 1.3 km where you turn left and walk along a forestry track. After a short distance the track forks and you bear right following the track uphill for another 900 m until the dam and reservoir come into view and you arrive at a path, on the right, leading down to the dam.

For the more challenging direct route, leave the road through the gate and walk north across the fields for 200 m until you arrive at a wire fence with a stile. Cross the stile into the next field and continue north. This field is wet and overgrown with reeds. Continue north across the field and descend towards conifer woodland, making for the left-hand side of a small stone wall in front of the wood. As you reach the wall you will find a stile previously hidden by reeds. This bottom corner of the field is waterlogged. Cross the stile and the small stream beyond. The path is not clear but from the stream you make your way north and climb up through woodland for 250 m until you reach a forestry track. Go straight across the track and continue north, through the trees, for another 400 m until you emerge and join the easy route near the dam.

Follow the footpath down to the dam and cross it to the picnic area. The dam was started in 1909 and the lake supplies Welsh homes with 5 million gallons of water a day. Local wildlife includes Black Grouse and Red Squirrels. From the picnic area retrace your steps over the dam and continue west along the footpath following the shoreline for 800 m until you reach a forestry track. The path around the lake is the circular Llwybr Alwen Trail. Turn left along the forestry track and walk south-west.

After 200 m the track turns left and you walk south for 140 m to a crossroads. Go straight across and walk 350 m until you reach a junction with a smaller track going south-east, which you take. There is a metal gate after a short distance. Go through the gate and continue with the stone wall on your left. You soon reach a cottage and two more gates leading to a tarmac lane. Continue south along the lane.

Walk along the lane for 1 km until you reach a metal gate. Go through the gate and continue straight on for another 300 m to a junction, where you go straight on. Keep following the lane as it meanders south for another 1.25 km until you reach a T-junction where you turn left and walk east.

Go 600 m along the road until you reach a stile leaving the road on your right. Go over the stile and walk downhill across the field to the metal gate at the bottom. Go through the gate and turn left, walking through a gap in the wall after which you turn right and walk towards the bottom of the field. Cross the stile at the bottom of the field and head uphill, walking south-east until you reach a metal gate leading to a road. Turn right along the road and walk the short distance back to the centre of the village.

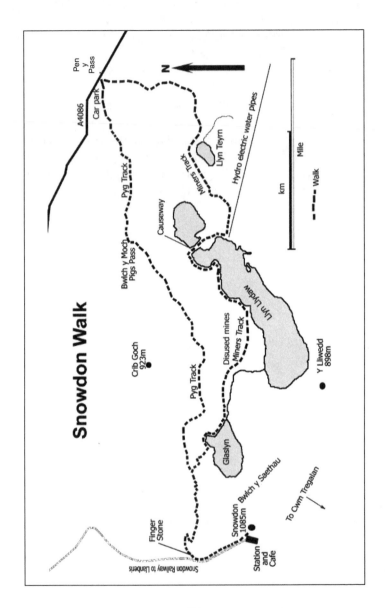

Snowdon Walk

N

Pen y Pass

A4086

Car park

Pyg Track

Bwlch y Moch
Pigs Pass

Crib Goch
923m

Pyg Track

Miners' Track

Llyn Teyrn

Hydro electric water pipes

Causeway

Llyn Llydaw

Disused mines
Miners Track

Y Lliwedd
898m

Glaslyn

Finger Stone

Bwlch y Saethau

Snowdon
1085m

Station
and
Cafe

To Cwm Tregalan

Snowdon Railway to Llanberis

km

Mile

- - - - Walk

7

The Death of Arthur

It was the winter of life. Camelot was no more and the high ideals of valour and courage were nothing more than tales told by old men to eager children. Arthur, king of the Britons, old and tired now, had vanished. The Knights of the Round Table were dispersed across Europe, searching for the Holy Grail. Darkness and evil permeated the land.

Arthur's evil son Mordred wanted the throne and, after years of searching, his spies finally located Arthur and sent word to the usurper. Arthur was at the city of Tregalan, hidden in Cwm Tregalan in the kingdom of Gwynedd, with just a small retinue of men led by ever-faithful Sir Bedevere.

Mordred was eager to claim the crown and had no love for his father. He gathered his army and marched on Snowdonia to seize power. Errant knights and outlaws of every kind flocked to Mordred's banner, greedy for plunder and the spoils of war. As they advanced, Mordred's army pillaged and burned. Word reached Arthur of the advancing throng and, old as he was, he knew that he had to give battle. Mordred had to be stopped.

A weary Arthur gathered together his small band of warriors, mainly old knights and boys and rode out to meet Mordred in mortal combat. Expecting Arthur, Mordred sent archers to hide in the mountains with orders to let Arthur by while the rest of his army camped at Pen y Pass. His plan was to trap Arthur between Llyn Llydaw and Snowdon and kill every man with him. He wanted no survivors to talk of heroism or martyrs.

It was a cold damp winter morning as Arthur and his men marched down the valley past Llyn Llydaw to confront Mordred's army by the bank of Llyn Teyrn. The battle was fierce and no quarter was given. Men that fell wounded were slain. Outnumbered, Arthur's small band was forced to retreat. Slowly they fell back along the valley towards Snowdon, leaving a trail of dead as they went.

As they pressed on, Mordred's soldiers tripped and fell over their fallen comrades. Friend and foe alike sank into the slimy mud. The battle raged throughout the day, until it was nearly dark and a damp mist enveloped the exhausted men. Still they fought. Now Arthur had just a few men left. They were trapped below the great mountain, Snowdon. Sensing victory, Mordred pushed his way to the front of the fight. He saw Arthur, bloody and wounded, surrounded by his enemies. Hatred and greed filled Mordred's heart and he charged at Arthur eager to kill his own father.

Arthur raised his sword, Excalibur, and with a mighty blow cleaved Mordred's head from his body. As Mordred fell, a flight of arrows rained down on Arthur and, clutching his sword, he fell to the ground. The archers, hidden at Bwlch y Saethau (the pass of arrows) behind Arthur and his men, had done their evil work.

Without a leader, Mordred's army had no cause and the fighting quickly stopped. Loyal Sir Bedevere helped Arthur from the battlefield and listened as the dying king whispered his last command.

'Take Excalibur and throw it far into the lake,' croaked Arthur. Sir Bedevere took the King's sword to throw it into Llyn Llydaw, but he could not. Twice he returned to Arthur asking the king to keep the mighty blade, and twice Arthur commanded him to throw it into the lake. Finally, overcome with grief, Sir Bedevere cast Excalibur far into the lake. As he watched the water parted

The summit of Snowdon viewed from the finger stone

and a silky white hand emerged, holding aloft the sword that had been Arthur's symbol of authority and strength since the day he had pulled it from the stone. Slowly the hand and the sword sank into the copper-green water.

Sir Bedevere looked back at his king. Arthur was dead. It was dark now and a fine rain was falling. Silently, a boat glided across the lake out of the darkness. In it sat three maidens dressed in black velvet. Torches flared and spluttered in the damp. They carefully and silently placed Arthur's body in the funeral barge and, without a sound, the maidens, the boat and Arthur glided into the darkness and the Otherworld.

Quietly, Sir Bedevere and the few remaining men who had fought so valiantly climbed Mount Lliwedd and vanished from history. There they remain, deep in the mountain, waiting for Arthur to return from the green waters of Llyn Llydaw, ready to lead them once again.

Snowdon Walk

As well as being the second highest point in Great Britain, Snowdon (*Yr Wyddfa*) has the advantage of being accessible in a variety of ways, including a railway that will carry you right to the top. Weather permitting, the views are breathtaking. Snowdonia has been a National Park since 1951. The Snowdon Walk is one of the more strenuous in this series but can be walked in ways that suit most levels of fitness and ability. The walk I have described is a circular one starting from Pen y Pass with a detour to include climbing up to the summit. The summit at 1085 m (3560 ft) can be omitted to shorten the distance and reduce the climb by 345 m (1130 ft). An alternative strategy is to complete the climb, descend using the mountain railway, and then catch a Sherpa bus from Llanberis back to the car park at Pen y Pass.

The Sherpa buses run around the mountain throughout the year (but you may want to check the timetables before your walk) between various starting points, making it practical to ascend one way then return using a different route and still be able to get back to your car. For less energetic walkers, it is possible to leave

Ordnance Survey map number 115 grid reference SH 647 555
Latitude = 53.0806, Longitude = -4.0209
Lat = 53 degrees, 4.8 minutes North
Long = 4 degrees, 1.3 minutes West

Length	11.69 km – 7.26 miles
Maximum height	1085.24 m
Minimum height	363.55 m
Height ascended	921.46 m
Navigation	Easy
Difficulty	Hard
Estimated time	6 hours 37 minutes

Looking east from the summit: the Pyg Track is on the left and the Miners' Track lower on the right

Looking north from the summit

Pen y Pass car park using the Miners' Track past Llyn Llydaw and walk up to the base of Snowdon, before returning by the same route. This is a good path with great views and involves very little climbing until you reach the top of the track.

Pen y Pass is a pay and display car park with toilets. There are also toilets and refreshments available in the café at the summit of Snowdon. Pen y Pass is popular and often full up by 8 am or 9 am, so an early start is recommended. Don't be tempted to park on the road, where you will get a fixed penalty ticket. If the car park is full there are alternatives, including Nant Peris car park at the bottom of Llanberis Pass from where you can catch a Sherpa 'park and ride' bus back to Pen y Pass.

Before you start, check the weather, pack some refreshments, dress appropriately and allow plenty of time, particularly if you intend to climb to the top of the mountain.

The alternative and more gentle walk (not described here) is to start from Pen y Pass and walk along the Miners' Track to Llyn Llydaw and the foot of Snowdon, returning to the car park the same way. The return distance for this walk is 6 miles, but you can shorten it as you wish. There are some great views of Snowdon from the lake, and the pathway is relatively flat.

The Circular Walk
Leave Pen y Pas car park using the footpath on the south-west corner clearly signposted 'Pyg Track'. This pathway is named either after Bwlch y Moch (Pig's Pass), which it travels through, or the 'pyg' (black tar) that used to be carried along it to the copper mines or – more probable – P(en) Y G(wryd) path, after the hotel at Penygwryd. The path begins to climb in a series of stairways towards Crib Goch, the mountain you can see immediately ahead of you. This is not Snowdon, as a lot of people imagine as they

start to walk the Pyg Track.

After you have travelled 1.6 km you will reach Bwlch y Moch pass. Going over the pass, you will see Llyn Llydaw ahead of you in the valley below and will come to a junction in the path. Excalibur lies somewhere at the bottom of the lake. Across the valley beyond the lake is Y Lliwedd, the mountain where Sir Bedevere and his men are hidden, waiting for Arthur's return. Ignore the right turn signposted 'Crib Goch'. This is a mountain ridge walk to Snowdon and not recommended for novice walkers or during windy weather. Instead, continue ahead over a stile with a blue plaque inscribed 'Pyg Track to Snowdon Summit'. Continue along the Pyg Track with the lake on your left. The footpath is well maintained here but, as you draw level with the end of the lake, the path deteriorates until you find yourself scrambling over bare rock where the route is barely visible.

Walk across the rock, keeping slightly uphill, and look for wear that has made the pathway smooth, and shinier than the surrounding rock surface. Snowdon is now directly ahead and, depending on the visibility, you will get a good view of the summit. In the valley below the summit is Glaslyn, a dark green lake, where the water is discoloured with copper residue from the old mine workings. Bwlch y Saethau is between the lake and Snowdon.

The Pyg Track now turns right and then left following the contour of Crib Goch, the mountain you are walking around. After 600 m you will reach a junction with a path coming up from the valley on your left. This is the point where the Pyg and the Miners' Tracks join, and the path on your left is your return route to Pen y Pas. The meeting point of the tracks is marked with a large flat standing stone. If you don't want to climb to the summit turn left, down the Miners' Track; otherwise, continue along the Pyg Track as it begins to climb more steeply.

You get fabulous 360-degree views from the
trig point at the summit of Snowdon

The path now zig-zags as it climbs a more difficult section of the walk until you arrive at a second standing stone known, because of its shape, as the 'finger stone'. As you reach the finger stone you will get your first views of the north Wales coastline and beyond. Turn left and continue uphill. This is the final part of the ascent and the path runs alongside the mountain railway until it reaches the small station at the top.

The trig point on the summit includes bearings and distances of distant landmarks. On a day with good visibility, usually when there is high atmospheric pressure and no cloud, it is possible to see high points that are over 100 miles away.

Cwm Tregalan, the valley where the ancient city of Tregalan was, can be seen looking south from the top of Snowdon and can be reached using the Watkin Path. It is a particularly beautiful valley and the site of a famous speech made by Prime Minister

Gladstone when he was eighty-two years old.

While you are at the summit you can also visit the new café that was opened in June 2009 and cost £8.35m. This replaced the old one, which had been described by Prince Charles as 'The highest slum in Wales'.

The descent from the top of Snowdon is made by retracing your steps back to the junction with the Miners' Track, and following it as it drops down into the valley and Glaslyn. As you reach the lake turn left past redundant mine buildings, and follow the pathway alongside the shore until you reach Afon Glaslyn, where the path turns and heads down the valley with the river on your right.

As you descend, the track improves taking you past disused mine workings and down to Llyn Llydaw. Walk along the track alongside the lake on your right and follow it past the ancient skeletons of the Britannia Copper Mines that were finally abandoned in 1917, until you come to a causeway dividing the lake. Cross the causeway and follow the track as it leaves the lake adjacent to a pipeline taking the water to produce hydroelectric power 500 ft lower down in the Glaslyn valley.

The Miners' Track now continues its gentle descent and as you pass Llyn Teyrn on your right you will get a good view of the Glaslyn valley looking east. 500 m past Llyn Teyrn the track turns north and you have a further 800 m of easy walking back to the car park at Pen y Pas.

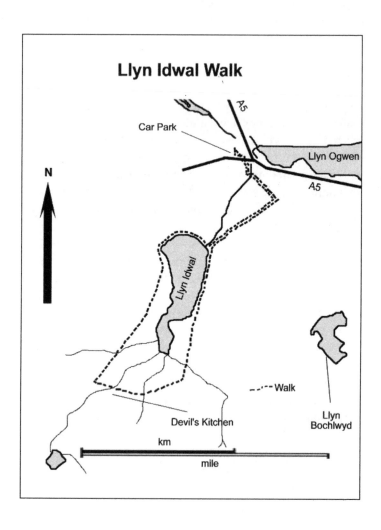

Llyn Idwal Walk

Car Park

A5

Llyn Ogwen

A5

N

Llyn Idwal

Llyn Bochlwyd

Devil's Kitchen

- · - · - Walk

km

mile

8

Prince Idwal

At the beginning of the twelfth century the kingdom of Gwynedd was ruled by Owain ap Cynan. Owain, whose royal title was Owain Gwynedd, had nineteen sons, but the fairest by far was Idwal. The other princes raced each other, played rough games of war, and grew strong. Idwal, however, was not like his boisterous brothers. He would sit for hours quietly reading or listening to the court musicians as they practiced. Sometimes he would wander alone in the gardens, admiring flowers and singing sweet melodies.

Owain realised that Idwal would never be a warrior, and that saddened him. But as the boy grew his father saw that he was intelligent and kind to all. The king admired Idwal's perfect features and placid temperament. Some called the boy weak, but Owain was proud of Idwal.

When the king of Powys attacked the kingdom of Gwynedd, men were called to arms to drive off the invader. Eager to prove their strength in battle, the king's sons pleaded with their father to go to war. The king agreed, since it was their duty, as princes, to earn their place with deeds of bravery in battle. But what, the king wondered, should he do with Idwal?

'Send him to Nefydd Hardd,' suggested a courtier. 'Nefydd is a great musician and will teach Idwal to play the harp.'

'Where does Nefydd Hardd live?' asked the King.

'High in the mountains by Llyn Ogwen. No harm will come to Idwal there,' replied the courtier.

Nefydd Hardd (*hardd*: 'beautiful') was leader of one of the fifteen tribes of Wales. The king agreed to the plan and Idwal was sent to the house of Nefydd Hardd high in the mountains, where he would be safe from the king's enemies. Nefydd Hardd greeted Idwal and introduced Dunawd, his son, to the royal guest. 'You will be brothers. I will educate you together,' he cried and squeezed Idwal's hand.

Idwal took well to the music and poetry lessons from his new tutor. Each day the young men sat together as Nefydd Hardd instructed them. Idwal learned quickly but Dunawd, who was slow-witted, struggled. Nefydd Hardd was a vain man. Often he had boasted to his friends how clever his son Dunawd was, and had sung in praise of the boy's good looks. 'He will grow up to be as brilliant and good-looking as me,' he had said.

But as he watched the two boys together he grew envious of Idwal's handsome face and resentful of Idwal's sharp mind. Only a fool could fail to see that Dunawd was a plain, stupid oaf by comparison, and Nefydd Hardd was no fool.

As the weeks passed, Nefydd Hardd grew to despise the prince sheltering under his roof, and his dull son grew jealous of their visitor. Idwal could feel the jealousy and hatred but being a kindly youth, with no malice in him, he responded with courtesy and compassion. Idwal's good manners infuriated Nefydd Hardd and his son even more.

One dark afternoon Nefydd Hardd sent for his son. 'Dunawd, you should take Prince Idwal for a walk. Show him the lake at the head of the valley,' said Nefydd Hardd.

'But father, it will be dark soon and there are storm clouds on the mountain,' replied Dunawd.

'Take Idwal to the ridge above the lake but be careful that you don't slip. The path can be dangerous when it's wet,' said Nefydd Hardd.

86

Looking up from Llyn Idwal at the path that goes diagonally up the mountain; the Devil's Kitchen is on the right at the top

Dunawd looked at his father. The old man was grinning.

'And what if Idwal slips and falls into the lake?' Dunawd asked.

'That would be a terrible accident, which would be no one's fault,' replied his father.

It had started to rain as the two young men left the house. Dunawd marched ahead. 'Come on,' he cried. 'There is something I want you to see.'

Idwal followed behind, the rain streaming down his face. They walked around the lake towards the mountain. Their legs sank deep into the soft peat. Dunawd strode on into the gathering gloom. When they reached a narrow ledge he stopped.

'Here it is, look,' he yelled.

Idwal hurried to join his companion.

'What is it?' asked the prince, looking around.

'See the lake below, it's your destiny,' laughed Dunawd and

shoved Idwal off the ledge.

Prince Idwal screamed as he fell into the lake but the wind snatched the sound from his lips and carried the plaintive cry up into the mountains. Dunawd walked back to the house alone.

Owain returned from the war and searched for his son, but Idwal's body was never found. He suspected foul play but had no proof that Nefydd Hardd or his son Dunawd had murdered the prince. Even so, he seized Nefydd Hardd's lands and banished him and his son, Dunawd, from the kingdom.

The evil pair never admitted the crime but, in 1170, when Owain Gwynedd died, Rhun ap Nefydd Hardd, younger brother of Dunawd, returned to Gwynedd and built a church at Llanrwst in penitence for the foul murder done by his family.

The lake where Idwal drowned is named after him, and it is said that no bird will fly across the water where the evil deed was done. It is also said that sometimes, when the wind blows from the west, you can hear the echo of the young Prince's scream as he fell into the icy water ...

Llyn Idwal with Pen yr Ole Wen mountain behind

Llyn Idwal Walk

The Llyn Idwal walk takes you around the beautiful Idwal valley, which was created by a glacier pushing north, before being cut by a second glacier below where the lake now sits. The resulting scenery is spectacular. In a survey conducted in 2005 Cwm Idwal was voted as the seventh greatest wonder in the United Kingdom. The area doubled as the Khyber Pass in the film *Carry on up the Khyber*, and has featured more recently in episodes of *Doctor Who*. Most of the path is a clearly defined stone pavement, but some sections on the southern end of the walk involve large stone steps and clambering across rocks – not good if you wear bifocal glasses or have wobbly knees! There is also a stream in a narrow rock gully to cross, where extra care needs to be taken, particularly when there has been heavy rain. However, the views and magic of the valley make this a worthwhile walk. The walk starts from a National Trust car park located at the western end of Llyn Ogwen, on the A5, ten miles west of Betws-y-coed. The car park is pay and display, with toilets, a small information centre and a kiosk selling drinks and snacks. This is a popular tourist area and the car park fills up early in the morning during peak holiday times.

Ordnance Survey map number 115 grid reference SH 648 604
Latitude = 53.1235, Longitude = -4.0202
Lat = 53 degrees, 7.4 minutes North
Long = 4 degrees, 1.2 minutes West

Length	4.96 km – 3.08 miles
Maximum height	584.45 m
Minimum height	295.50 m
Height ascended	315.17 m
Navigation	Easy
Difficulty	Hard
Estimated time	2 hours 33 minutes

Leave the car park along the stone path that is on the left of the toilet block, so that you are walking south-east. After a short distance the path forks and you continue following the left path signposted 'Llyn Idwal Path'. This takes you over two stone bridges. Continue south east for 500 m where the path turns right taking you south-west and continues to climb up the valley.

As you climb, Llyn Ogwen will come into view behind you, and on your right you will have long distance views along Nant Ffrancon. This large valley with curved sides is a good example of a glacial valley, and was the route chosen by Thomas Telford when he built the London to Holyhead turnpike road (now the A5), between 1810 and 1826. To avoid steep gradients the road was cut along the sides of the valley, making it more difficult to build but a much faster route.

Continue south-west for 500 m with the river on your right, until you arrive at the lake that is Llyn Idwal. Turn left and follow the path along the shore.

Ahead of you is the valley surrounded by the Glyder mountains, against which the glacier pushed as it grew. Glyder Fawr is the tallest of these at 999 m. On the far slopes at the end of the lake you will see a crevice that is known as the Devil's Kitchen (*Twll Du*). The steam sometimes seen rising from here is, according to legend, made by the devil as he boils his evil brews. Our walk passes just under the Devil's Kitchen before returning down the west side of the valley. For more intrepid walkers there is a route, not described here, through the Devil's Kitchen and over the Glyderau.

Walk along the side of the lake for 350 m to a metal gate where the path starts to climb away from the lake shore. After 500 m it turns to the right and starts to climb more steeply, taking you south-west for 250 m. This section of climb is over larger uneven steps. Look at the rock formation on your left as you walk and notice how the grain has been tilted to an acute angle by volcanic action. Cwm Idwal is popular with climbers who test their skills on the mountains here. The Devil's Kitchen is particularly good for ice climbing in the winter months. In the 1950s and 60s Cwm Idwal was the site for reunions of the first successful Everest Mountaineering Team lead by John Hunt in 1953. It was the ninth British attempt on the mountain; on 29 May 1953 New Zealander Edmund Hillary and Sherpa Tenzing Norgay were the first men to reach the summit.

The path now follows the wall of the valley and turns west as you continue to climb. After 150 m you will reach a stream rushing down through a narrow gorge, which you have to scramble across taking care not to slip on the wet rock. From the stream the path climbs west for a distance until you arrive at a group of large boulders. Turn left heading up the mountain for a short distance before turning right again where the path forks. You are now just below the Devil's Kitchen; the left-hand path, which is not our route, leads up through the Kitchen and over the mountain.

This is the highest point of the walk and you have now climbed 315 m from the car park. Do the walk just twenty-eight times and you will have climbed the height of Everest, from sea level! Looking north from here you will have stunning views of Llyn Idwal and Llyn Ogwen below it.

After a short distance the path turns north-east and begins to descend. Initially, the descent is steep but as you get lower and nearer the lake the rate of fall gets easier. Keep walking north-east for 1 km until you reach a stone wall with a metal gate. Go through the gate and turn right, walking east along the pebble shoreline, which you follow until it ends and you rejoin the path for a short distance.

The path will bring you to a metal gate and footbridge leading to the path that brought you up to the lake earlier. Here, you turn left and retrace your steps downhill, back to the car park.

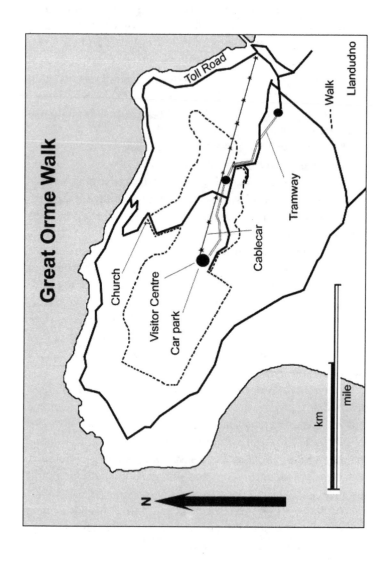

Great Orme Walk

Toll Road

Tramway

Cablecar

Church

Visitor Centre

Car park

- - - Walk

Llandudno

N

km

mile

9

Prince Madog Sails to America

In memory of Prince Madog,
a Welsh explorer, who landed on the shores
of Mobile Bay in 1170
and left behind, with the Indians, the Welsh language.

Plaque erected in Mobile, Alabama, USA in 1953

Prince Madog was the son of Owain Gwynedd, prince of Gwynedd. Owain, not content with just two wives (the maximum allowed according to Welsh law at that time), also kept four mistresses. He sired nineteen sons, many of whom, including Madog, were illegitimate. According to custom, all the children were openly acknowledged as Owain's. When he died in 1169, rivalries between his sons eager to take the throne quickly escalated into open warfare.

Being illegitimate, Madog was not a contender for the crown, and unwilling to take sides in the increasingly bloody fights, he resolved to escape from Wales. Two stout ships were fitted out ready for a voyage. The *Gorn Gwynant* and the *Pedr Sant* had been built from sturdy oak trees hewn from the forest of Nant Gwynant. Prince Madog had sailed in them before and was a skilled navigator already famous for his adventures.

The prince was a popular leader and men were eager to crew his ships. The ships departed from a quay on the Afon Ganol, at what is now Rhos-on-Sea, and set sail west. They stopped at Lundy Island, where Prince Rhirid, one of Madog's brothers, joined them. From Lundy the two vessels sailed on past Ireland, steering steadily west, heading for the edge of the known world.

The fight for the throne of Gwynedd continued. Owain's designated son and heir, Hywel ab Owain Gwynedd, fell at the battle of Pentraeth, killed by his half-brothers Dafydd and Rhodri. The war continued and other brothers were killed in battle or murdered, until only Dafydd and Rhodri remained strong enough to claim the crown. Eventually, the kingdom was divided between Dafydd and Rhodri and an uneasy peace was established. Another generation would pass before the kingdom of Gwynedd was finally reunified under Llywelyn the Great.

Madog had almost been forgotten when, years later, he returned with a strange tale to tell. He had crossed a great ocean to a distant land, a land inhabited by friendly people with dark skins who welcomed him and his crew, a land where, if you were hungry, you just had to reach up and pluck sweet fruits from the trees. He told of rivers that were full of fish, and great plains covered with herds of huge beasts the natives called buffalo.

Some of Madog's crew had remained behind in the strange land and Madog announced, at once, that he would return across the great ocean to join his men. He invited others, who might want to start a new life, to come. Ten ships were prepared and quickly filled, ready for the long voyage. Once more Madog sailed away to the west.

After a long and dangerous journey, they landed at a place we now call Mobile, Alabama. From Mobile the ships travelled inland along mighty rivers. Mandan Indians guided the Welshmen. The settlers built forts to protect themselves against unfriendly tribes.They taught their Mandan guides to speak Welsh, and how to fish using coracles. The Welshmen took native wives and, over

Great Orme Tramway and the cable car:
the easy ways to get to the summit

the years, the Mandans and the Welshmen merged to become one tribe.

Madog never returned to Wales, but there is ample evidence of his arrival in America.

In 1608 explorer Peter Wynne discovered a tribe in Virginia calling themselves Monacan Indians and wrote that they spoke 'Welch'. In 1669 Reverend Morgan Jones was captured by a tribe called the Doeg. When he conversed with them in Welsh they understood his meaning. He stayed with the Doeg for several months before being released and returning to the British colonies. In 1799, Governor John Sevier of Tennessee reported the discovery of six skeletons wearing brass armour bearing the Welsh coat of arms.

A mound and stone fortification called the Devil's Backbone exists fourteen miles upstream from Louisville, Kentucky, built about the same time as Prince Madog arrived using a design similar to castles that existed in north Wales. Cherokee Indian tradition refers to a tribe of 'fair-skinned moon-eyed' people, known as Modoc, who built a stone castle on Fort Mountain, Georgia. In 1832 German ethnologist, Prince Maximilian of Wied-Neuwied, travelled up the Missouri and across the Great Plains. He studied the Mandan language and made a comparison list of common Welsh and Mandan words. In 1841, the painter George Catlin painted Mandan Indians fishing using a round boat refered to as a 'bull boat'. Its design was the same as the Welsh coracle.

Other evidence exists, including DNA and radiocarbon dating, to support the fact that Madog discovered and settled in America more than 300 years before Christopher Columbus arrived. In 1738 French traders visited nine Mandan villages along the Heart River, containing 15,000 inhabitants. The Mandans had become a great Indian nation and had prospered and spread up into the Great Plains of America.

Sadly, in 1837, the Mandan tribe was infected with smallpox by the crew of a visiting boat. The disease tore through the nation and only 125 Mandans survived the epidemic. The United States government then merged the Mandans with other Indian tribes and the last full-blooded Mandan died in 1971. How much of Madog's Welsh blood ran in his veins we shall never know.

The plaque commemorating the voyage of Prince Madog was damaged by a hurricane in 1979 and removed, for safe keeping, by the US military. Since then, the Alabama Welsh Society has been campaigning for it to be replaced, in its original position, in honour of the first European to discover America.

I have dwelt longer on the history and customs of these

people than I have or shall on any other tribe... because I have found them a very peculiar people. From the striking peculiarities in their personal appearance, in their customs, traditions, and language, I have been led conclusively to believe that they are a people of a decidedly different origin from that of any other tribe in these regions.

George Catlin 1796–1872
American Artist

Great Orme Walk

The Great Orme (*Gogarth*) is a large limestone headland near Llandudno. The word Orme is Viking for serpent, and the headland would have looked like a giant sea serpent from Madog's tiny vessels as they sailed away. Its small cousin on the other side of the town is Little Orme (*Trwyn y Fuwch*) and it was at Rhos (*Llandrillo-yn-rhos*), just beyond Little Orme, that Madog set sail on his epic voyage. Great Orme can be reached by driving 20 miles north from Betws-y-coed or 8 miles west from Colwyn Bay. This is a walk with spectacular views of Conwy and its castle, Anglesey and the Victorian resort town Llandudno. Our walk starts at the summit of Great Orme, which can be reached by car, along Marine Drive. There is a toll charge for using Marine Drive but your toll ticket also acts as a car parking ticket in the pay and display car park. Alternatively you can reach the summit using either the cable car system, starting from Happy Valley in Llandudno, or the tramway, which also travels up from the town. There are toilets, shops, a café and visitor centre at the summit.

Ordnance Survey map number 115 grid reference SH 765 833
Latitude = 53.3323, Longitude = -3.8551
Lat = 53 degrees, 19.9 minutes North
Long = 3 degrees, 51.3 minutes West

Length	6.38 km – 3.96 miles
Maximum height	194.77 m
Minimum height	99.88 m
Height ascended	198.96 m
Navigation	Easy
Difficulty	Moderate
Estimated time	2 hours 38 minutes

Leave the car park through the vehicle entrance and turn right so that you are walking south-west down a steep slope with a wall on your right. Ahead are views of Penmaenmawr and the enormous old limestone quarries that scar the mountains. Further west you will see Anglesey and Ynys Seiriol (*Puffin Island*). On a clear day it is also possible to see the Isle of Man.

Turn right at the corner of the wall and walk north, keeping the wall on your right. After a short distance, look back to your left to see a spectacular view of Conwy castle, the estuary and Deganwy. Continue walking north-west for 1 km until you reach another corner and a cairn where the wall turns north-east. Follow the footpath along the wall. Generally, it keeps near the wall but in places moves away, taking you across centuries old limestone pavements.

Looking north-east you will see ranks of wind turbines spinning lazily in the wind or standing idly like silent sentinels. This is Gwynt y Môr wind farm. It comprises 200 wind turbines covering an area of 50 square miles and generating enough electricity for up to 500,000 homes. During a heated public enquiry in 2006 supporters of the project claimed that the wind farm would become a tourist attraction, while one local resident described the wind farm proposed as a 'visual obscenity.' The people of Llandudno voted against the building of the wind farm, claiming that it would destroy the tourism industry, but were overruled.

After 500 m the wall and footpath turns right again and you walk south-east. After a short distance the path becomes a track, which you follow for 900 m. As you proceed along the track you pass the remains of a Roman well on your left, and the summit complex will be on your right.

When you reach the end of the track turn left and walk downhill along the road for 320 m, passing the entrance to the new cemetery and leaving the road through the second stone gateway leading into the churchyard. This is St Tudno's church. St Tudno is the patron saint of Llandudno and is celebrated in the town on 5 June each year. He was also, it is claimed, one of Madog 's nineteen siblings. The original church was rebuilt in the twelfth century, and in the tradition of St Tudno services are held both inside the church and outside in the churchyard. There is a pulpit and seating for the congregation in the churchyard. Dogs are welcome at the services, even if they take part in the singing!

During your walk, you may see wild goats grazing. These are Kashmiri goats, from Northern India and there is a herd of them living on Great Orme. Originally, in about 1880, a pair were released on Great Orme from Queen Victoria's royal herd at Windsor. Because of their isolation on Great Orme for over 100 years, the goats have since evolved into heavier animals with less shaggy coats and larger horns. Over the years, numbers have been

St Tudno's church

controlled with culling, but more recently birth control implants are used; being considered more humane. Goats taken from Great Orme are used as regimental mascots in the British army.

Leave the church through the gateway with the stone cross on the top of the roof, cross the road and follow the footpath signposted to the 'Ski Centre' and 'Llandudno' so that you are walking south-east. After a short distance you pass through a kissing gate and arrive at Powell's Well. The Powell family farmed here at one time and struggled to find sufficient water to give their animals. One day, according to the story, they prayed at St Tudno's church, and as they returned home a spring rose up from the barren ground. It has never run dry since.

Just past the well the path turns left and through another kissing gate, so that you are walking east. After 100 m the path widens into a track leading to a white farmhouse. Go through the double metal gates at the front of the house and walk uphill for 60 m to a junction and the next kissing gate. Proceed through the gate and turn left following the 'To Town' sign. 15 m further on, the path forks and you bear left. As you climb up the slope Little Orme comes into view ahead. After 400 m the path turns to the right and Llandudno comes into view. Rhos, from where Madog set sail for America, is on the coast just past Little Orme. The stone quay beside which his ships were berthed before they sailed is now part of a private garden that you cannot visit, but there is a plaque, which reads:

PRINCE MADOG SAILED FROM HERE
ABER-KERRIK-GWYNAN 1170 A.D.
AND LANDED AT MOBILE, ALABAMA
WITH HIS SHIPS
GORN, GWYNANT AND PEDR SANT

Continue downhill to a junction and turn right, following the path signposted 'summit' and 'Copper mines', so that you are walking south-west. The path then forks and you bear left, aiming for the cable car gantry at the top of the slope. This part of the walk gives excellent views over Llandudno. At the top of the slope you pass under the cable cars that zip holidaymakers from Happy Valley to the summit. The cable car system was opened in 1969 and at the time was the longest in Britain. The path passes to the left of the gantry and then descends towards the tramway.

The modern blue building ahead of you is the tram shed and engine house. Great Orme Tramway uses a system of cables and pulleys under the track, to pull the trams along, similar to the trams of San Francisco. When you reach the tracks, turn left, cross over the tramway and walk a short distance down the road to a turning on the right before the first house. The lane has a 'dead end' sign.

After 100 m the lane forks and you bear right along Pyllau Road following the 'To the summit' footpath sign. The lane quickly becomes a track and you continue though a metal gate. On your right is a Bronze Age copper mine. The copper was mined and then mixed with tin to produce bronze, used for making weapons and utensils. The workings of the mine are extensive. So far over 6 km of underground prehistoric tunnels have been found. Just beyond the mine you reach a gate leading to Pen y Gogarth Nature Reserve, designated to protect vulnerable plant and insect species. Continue along the track until it joins the tarmac road and then leave the road to the left along the footpath signposted 'To summit'.

The footpath leads uphill and west. As you progress the footpath gets closer to the road, and then turns to the right, leading back to the car park at the summit.

*St Tudno's church, with the spectacular toll road
hugging the cliff beyond*

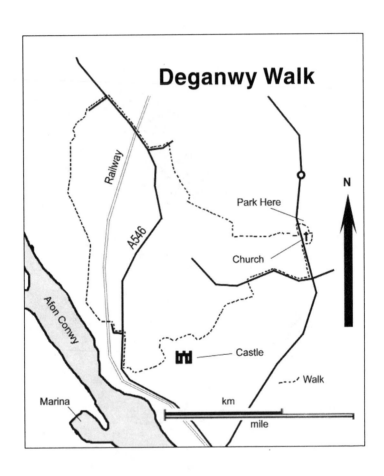

Deganwy Walk

Railway

A546

Park Here

Church

N

Afon Conwy

Castle

Walk

Marina

km

mile

10

Maelgwn Gwynedd and the Yellow Eye

Maelgwn Gwynedd, also known as Maelgwn Hir (*Maelgwn the Tall*) was prince of Gwynedd. He was a ruthless and ambitious man and had seized the throne from his uncle. Even after he became prince of Gwynedd, his ambition was not satisfied, for there were other kingdoms in Wales. Maelgwn was a jealous man. He wanted to be more powerful than the other princes. He wanted them all to pay homage to him.

He invited the other princes to meet him on the sands of Aberdyfi and to bring their thrones with them. There would be feasting and games, said the invitation. Maelgwn told them that they would be treated as honoured guests. The princes accepted the tempting offer and journeyed from across the land with their retainers. A great tent filled with carpets and tables laden with silver platters loaded with food was erected on the beach. Men at arms lined the shore, their weapons sparkling in the sunshine. Banners fluttered gaily in the breeze. Trumpeters welcomed the visitors, and fine words of greeting were exchanged between them.

The thrones were carried into the tent and the feast began. The princes chatted gaily. All agreed that the food and wines were fit for princes. Slowly, so as not to be obvious, Maelgwn turned the conversation to address a question. Which of the four princes was the most senior? The princes could not agree. One said they were equal, another claimed he was Chief Prince. The debate grew heated and the princes began to argue.

'My lords, there is a simple way we can settle the matter,' cried Maelgwn.

'How so?' asked the princes.

'The tide is out. Let us have our thrones moved to the edge of the water where we will sit. Whichever of us remains seated for the longest shall be honoured by all as Supreme Prince,' suggested Maelgwn.

It was agreed and the thrones were carried to the water's edge. The tide turned and the water started to rise. Before long the princes' feet were under water, but none of them moved. All wanted to be Chief Prince. The sea level continued to rise, covering their knees, but they did not move. Then, a strange thing happened. Maelgwn's throne began to lift up while the other kings' thrones slowly submerged. One by one they abandoned their thrones and waded away, leaving Maelgwn alone, floating on the water.

Concealed beneath his seat, Maelgwn had fitted pigs' bladders filled with air. The other princes had been tricked but, having given their solemn word, they were obliged to honour Maelgwn, and pledged their loyalty to him as their Chief Prince.

Maelgwn built a castle with a great tower on the twin hills of Deganwy known as the Vardre. He prayed with the monks, but quickly grew bored with their piety. 'Life is for living, and I shall live like a king,' he told his courtiers.

Maelgwn summoned musicians to entertain him and bards to write epic stories of his courage and goodness, but the songs and poems were lies, for the truth was that Maegwn was an evil man with a violent temper.

Maelgwn took Nesta, a princess from the north of England, as his wife, and gave her an ancient gold ring that had been worn by all the queens of Gwynedd. Later, as Nesta bathed in the river, the ring slipped from her wet finger and vanished into the water. Nesta was afraid of her husband and asked the Bishop of Llanelwy what she should do about the lost heirloom.

The Bishop considered her problem and invited the royal couple to join him for dinner. As the meal started the Bishop began to explain what had happened but, hearing that the ring was lost, Maelgwn flew into a rage. He accused his wife of adultery, paid for with the ring.

'Come, sire. That cannot be. Let us keep calm and consider the facts,' said the Bishop.

Maelgwn sat sullenly staring at his wife.

The original church built by Maelgwn Gwynedd was on this site

'Look at this fine salmon. It was caught this morning in the river,' said the Bishop. He cut and served the fish, giving the largest piece to Maelgwn.

'What is this?', cried Maelgwn, pointing at the salmon. Something glittered on the plate. It was the ring his wife had lost in the river. Maelgwn said nothing more – but he did not forgive his wife.

When Maelgwn's nephew visited Deganwy with a new bride, Maelgwn grew jealous. He wanted the young woman for himself. So he had his nephew murdered and seduced the young bride.

As time passed, Maelgwn's tyranny grew worse until all his people hated him. 'Who will rid us of this evil prince?' they cried.

A wise prophet and bard named Taleisin lived in the land.

'Tell us, wise man. Who will end Maelgwn's evil?' asked the people.

'A great beast will appear from the east. Its skin will be rotting and fetid. Its teeth and eyes will be yellow and its foul breath will whisper of death. This great putrid beast will avenge Maelgwn's evil and people will speak of the long sleep of Maelgwn in the church of Rhos,' said Taleisin.

The plague, which had started in Europe, spread quickly across England. It reached Gwynedd in 547, bringing misery and death to the people. Their skins ran with sores, their lungs filled with blood, their teeth and eyes turned yellow and their breath stank of death. Maelgwn feared for his life and, ignoring the cries for help from his courtiers as they died around him, he fled from the castle. The evil prince locked himself alone in the church at Llanrhos and prayed for sanctuary. The few loyal guards that remained waited outside, unsure of what to do. They knocked on the door of the church.

They shouted, 'Sire. What are your orders?'

'Go away,' yelled Maelgwn.

That night, as Maelgwn knelt praying, he heard a strange scratching at the door.

'Maelgwn, I have come for you,' whispered a voice from outside.

'Leave me alone,' cried Maelgwn.

'Maelgwn. Let me in,' whispered the voice.

Maelgwn picked up his candle and moved to the door.

He bent down and peered through the keyhole. A large yellow eye stared back at him ...

The guards returned the next morning but Maelgwn did not answer their calls.

'He is asleep. We dare not wake him,' said the guards and went away.

Days passed before they broke down the door. The evil prince's body was rotting and fetid. His teeth and eyes had turned yellow.

Maelgwn's body was taken to Ynys Seiriol and buried.

Taleisin's prophecy had come true.

Deganwy Walk

This is a walk that starts at the church of St Hilary, Llanrhos and takes you west to the ruin that was Deganwy castle and then drops down to the Conwy estuary, where it follows the coast heading north towards Llandudno before returning back to the church. From the castle you have views of Conwy Sands, Anglesey and Ynys Seiriol (*Puffin Island*), the reputed burial place of Maelgwn Gwynedd. Deganwy is 17 miles north of Betws-y-coed and 20 miles west of Prestatyn. Take the A546 into Deganwy and turn right onto the B5115. The church is 1.24 miles along this road. The best place to park is inside the entrance to the new cemetery just north of the church.

Ordnance Survey map number 115 grid reference SH 792 804
Latitude = 53.3068, Longitude = -3.8126
Lat = 53 degrees, 18.4 minutes North
Long = 3 degrees, 48.8 minutes West

Length	7.73 km – 4.80 miles
Maximum height	85.9 m
Minimum height	0 m
Height ascended	172.90 m
Navigation	Easy
Difficulty	Moderate
Estimated time	2 hours 35 minutes

Leave the car in the parking area just inside the gates and follow the short path leading south to the church. This is the site of the church built by Maelgwn, where he prayed to be spared from the plague. The church was rebuilt in 1865. Go through the churchyard and emerge at the main entrance. Walk south 400 m along the road, passing the old school on your right, and then turn right along Bryn Lupus Road.

Continue along Bryn Lupus Road for 600 m until you reach a driveway leading to Maes Dolau Farm on your left. Walk south along the driveway for 150 m, where the drive turns right and takes you between the farm buildings. The footpath leaves to the right, crosses a stile, and continues west for a further 200m along a narrow, tree-lined path.

The path then reaches a ladder stile and emerges into a field where you walk south-west for 180 m. As you walk up the field, turn and look back. In the far distance, if it is clear, you will see a group of oil and gas rigs near the horizon. These are part of the Lennox and Douglas complex located 24 km from the north Wales coast. There are estimated to be more than 150 million barrels of oil and 1.2 trillion cubic feet of gas in the field. With peak oil production expected to reach some 70,000 barrels per day, and gas capacity of 300 million cubic feet per day, the life of the field is expected to be more than twenty years.

Cross the next ladder stile at the top of the field and walk south-west, with the base of an old stone wall on your right. The footpath curves to the right around the top of the hill, so that you walk west 200 m to a stile with stone sheep pens on your left. From here you deviate slightly from the footpath and walk to the left around the hill. As you do so, earthworks and a stone pillar come into view between the summits of two hills. These are the remains of Deganwy castle.

Surveys of the ruin show that the castle covered both hills, and included a substantial tower, known as the Mansell Tower, on the smaller of the hills. Was it here that the evil Maelgwn seduced his nephew's bride?

A quarry inside the fortifications was lined with clay, probably to act as a water reservoir. Excavations of the site have found Roman coins. Records show that a Saxon army led by Ceolwulf of

Mercia attacked the fortress of Deganwy in 822. The castle was strengthened by the Normans and used as a base to attack the Welsh. In 1088 Robert of Rhuddlan was killed on the beach after attacking Welsh pirates as they tried to escape. The garrison was finally starved out by Llywelyn ap Gruffudd in 1263, and using stone taken from Deganwy Edward I built a new castle at Conwy, which could be re-supplied from the sea. According to one legend, the two hills on each side of the castle, known as the Vardre, were originally part of Ireland but broke off and floated across the sea before getting stuck in the sands of the Conwy estuary.

Leave the castle and walk downhill in a westerly direction. As you descend you rejoin the footpath and follow it to the left around the base of the hill until you are walking south and you reach a house with a large Victorian-style greenhouse just ahead. The footpath now turns right through a metal gate and along a narrow path down to a road. Turn right and continue downhill to Gannock Park Road, where you turn right and then left into York Road.

This will bring you to a junction with the main A546, where you turn right and walk 420 m north until you reach a turning on the left signposted to the beach. Turn left following the sign, and walk down through the parking area and over the footbridge that crosses the railway line. You now turn right and walk along the seafront path for 1.17 km. Ahead of you is the Great Orme, a headland just beyond Llandudno that is protected because of its historical and natural importance. During the Second World War the Royal Artillery moved their gunnery school here from Shoeburyness, and some of the concrete bunkers still exist further along the shore.

As you stroll along, watch out for various pieces of modern art scattered along the path. These include 'Mytilus Edulis' (mussels),

Coastal footpath with the Great Orme in the distance

'Pearls of the Earth', 'Precious Stones' and 'West Shore Shelter'. At one time the sands of the estuary were a major source of mussels, and a pearl from the estuary was set in the crown jewels during the reign of Charles II. In the nineteenth century the huge haul of 4 kg a week of pearls was shipped from here to London jewellers.

In case you miss the artwork while you are walking, towards the end of the seafront there are photographs and a sign describing what they all signify.

When you arrive at a car park and the West Shore Beach Café leave the path and turn right along Dale Street, then turn right and then left into Church Crescent. At the end of Church Crescent turn right and walk south-east for 450 m along the road, crossing the railway line once again, and arriving at a roundabout where you continue straight on.

After a short distance you turn left and walk 200 m along Hospital Road. Turn right along Ffordd yr Orsedd and leave the road along the footpath just to the right of the 'Goods Deliveries' sign at the hospital. The footpath joins a golf course fairway where you keep to the left-hand side, walking south-east for 210 m and aiming for a solitary tower on the hill ahead. As you climb, the path veers left away from the fairway and then turns right for a short distance before turning left again to a stile leading to a field.

Walk 300 m south-east across the field to a ladder stile where you continue straight on, ignoring the stile and footpath on your left. As you reach the brow of the hill Llanrhos church will come into view in the valley below. Walk down the field and leave it through a gate just to the right of a concrete water trough.

This brings you into a farmyard where, according to the Ordnance Survey map, in order to follow the footpath you turn right and then left between the barns and continue east, downhill through three further fields back to the church and our car. Unfortunately, when we walked the route, the farmyard was obstructed and we were obliged to turn left and follow the farm track back to the road, before turning right to walk the short distance back to our car.

Looking east to the Great Orme

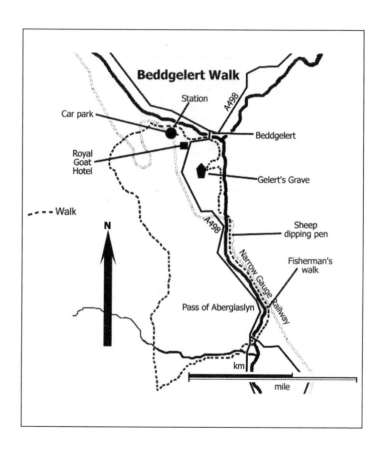

Beddgelert Walk

Station

Car park

A498

Beddgelert

Royal
Goat
Hotel

Gelert's Grave

- - - Walk

N

A498

Sheep
dipping pen

Fisherman's
walk

Narrow Gauge Railway

Pass of Aberglaslyn

km

mile

11

The Legend of Gelert

Prince Llywelyn the Great was a fine sportsman. His good humour and high spirits were known far and wide. Llywelyn's hall was a welcoming place, full of fun and friendship. He enjoyed his hunting and spent his days out with his horse and hounds. The biggest of his hounds was Gelert.

Llywelyn loved his animals and Gelert was his pride and joy. Never had a man owned such a fine hound. Gelert was the fastest and the bravest of his dogs and always the first at the kill. Gelert was fierce and brave. He was loyal and attentive. It was as if he knew his master's wishes and understood his moods. Of all the hounds Gelert was Llywelyn's favourite.

It was late autumn and the leaves had fallen from the trees. The woods were bare and the game easy to chase. Llywelyn took his horn and summoned the hounds with a long blast. They clamoured around his horse's hooves, baying with excitement. Their blood was up. It was time to hunt.

Llywelyn waved goodbye to his young wife and their baby then galloped out of the courtyard and away with his friends. The hounds followed close behind. The hunt went well and Llywelyn was pleased with the day. There would be a good table tonight with meat for all. They continued hunting until late in the afternoon and the light was fading when Llywelyn turned for home. Men, horses and dogs were all weary but elated with the day's sport.

As they trotted back from hunting, the men boasted about their brave deeds. They teased one and other and joked as they rode. The dogs followed silently, eager for home and their dinner; the reward for their effort. They did not bay now. Their work was done. Llywelyn looked around. He felt uneasy. Something was wrong. Who was missing? 'Where is Gelert?' he asked his friends. They stopped their idle chatter and searched for the great hound. He was nowhere to be seen.

'He was with us when we left the hall this morning,' said one.

'I have not seen Gelert at all today,' said another.

'He was with us a few minutes ago. I swear,' added another.

'Don't worry, he will turn up, my lord. Gelert is big enough to look after himself,' said another, cheerily.

They laughed and the hunting party rode on.

It was dark as they approached the great hall. The door was ajar and light shone through the doorway, illuminating the courtyard. 'This is strange,' thought Llywelyn. Suddenly, a piercing scream came from inside the hall. Llywelyn leapt from his horse and sprinted inside. His wife was slumped on a bench sobbing.

'What's wrong? Tell me,' he demanded.

His wife pointed to the back of the hall and their bedchamber. 'There! It's killed our baby!' she cried.

Llywelyn drew his sword and ran towards the bedchamber. The room was dim but he could see the crib in the light from the hall, behind him. It was empty. He could hear his wife weeping. His stomach turned and hate filled his heart. There was a noise near the crib. It was Gelert and the hound's jowls were red with blood. The dog sprang up to greet its master. Llywelyn raised his sword and ran the dog through.

Llywelyn returned to the hall and tried to comfort his grieving wife. Their hearts were broken and they sat together hugging and weeping. There was a whine from the bedchamber. Llywelyn leapt

The views from the mounntain above Beddgelert are spectacular

up with his sword and returned to finish the job. Then, a baby cried out, and his wife rushed into the bedchamber. Their child, hidden behind the bed, was alive and unharmed. Beside it lay the biggest wolf that had ever walked the lands of Gwynedd. The animal was dead. Killed by the faithful hound Gelert.

His wife took the child while Llywelyn cradled the dog's head in his arms. Gelert gave one last whimper and died.

The noble dog was buried and, as Llywelyn commanded, his grave was marked with a stone to record the bravery and loyalty he had shown. Llywelyn was consumed with guilt and sorrow. The great hall became a place of sadness and there were few visitors. For the rest of his life Llywelyn never hunted with the hounds, and those that knew him said he never laughed again.

Beddgelert Walk

The walk at Beddgelert includes stunning mountain views of Snowdonia, an ancient hill fort perched high above the town, a walk along the fisherman's path beside the river Glaslyn as it roars through the Pass of Aberglaslyn, and a visit to Gelert's grave. It involves quite a lot of climbing but you are well rewarded by the views. Beddgelert is located at the junction of the A498 and the A4085. It is 38 km north of Barmouth and 19 km south east of Caernarfon. The walk starts from the pay and display car park behind the Royal Goat Hotel. Toilets and refreshments are available in Beddgelert.

If the idea of a 7 km-long walk across the mountain sounds a bit strenuous you can do a shorter walk along the riverbank by Gelert's grave and return on the far side of the river, a total distance of 2 km. The path is flat with a tarmac surface, making it a very easy walk.

Ordnance Survey map number 115 grid reference SH 587 481
Latitude = 53.0119, Longitude = -4.1061
Lat = 53 degrees, 0.7 minutes North
Long = 4 degrees, 6.4 minutes West

Length	7.38 km – 4.58 miles
Maximum height	268.26 m
Minimum height	18.68 m
Height ascended	389.61 m
Navigation	Some sections on the mountain are not clearly marked
Difficulty	Hard
Estimated time	3 hours 34 minutes

Begin the walk by leaving the car park through a gate signposted to the railway station. This is the narrow-gauge Welsh Highland Railway, which starts from Caernarfon and snakes its way though

Afon Glaslyn; the fisherman's walk can be seen on the right of the river

the mountains, linking with the Ffestiniog Railway when it gets to Porthmadog. After a short distance, the tarmac path to the station turns sharp left and you leave it, continuing straight on along a stone track. When you reach a wooden gate turn left and under the railway line, where you turn again right and walk west until you reach a lane.

Turn left when you arrive at the lane and walk uphill across two unmanned railway crossings. Eventually the lane becomes a track and you reach Cwm Cloch and a converted cottage on the left. The footpath goes around the cottage and continues past an outbuilding with some tall stone steps at the side.

After another 100 m you will reach a second cottage which you pass on your left as the path continues south-east. Walk for

200 m until you reach a metal sign, fixed to the stone wall on your left, which reads 'Cwm Cloch', with an arrow pointing back the way you have come. Opposite the sign is a gate where the footpath continues south, and you climb through fields for 300 m until you reach a metal gate and a stone wall.

This gate will bring you onto the mountain, where you walk south-east for another 300 m before turning south again. You will have magnificent views of Beddgelert below you on your left and a panorama of Snowdonia all around. Some parts of the path are not marked, so a compass and map or GPS is needed.

Near the top of your climb you will reach a stone wall with a wooden gate, which you go through and head south down into the valley, aiming first for two piles of stones left as way-markers and then for a derelict farmhouse on the far side of the valley. The footpath continues along the left-hand side of the valley until you reach a stream. This is the start of the Afon Goch. Cross the stream and continue south. An ancient Iron Age hill fort named Pen-y-gaer will come into view below and ahead of you. This is your next objective. As you walk towards it the footpath becomes a track and passes a deserted farmhouse.

Just before you reach the fort, the footpath crosses a stream, turns left and heads downhill in a north-easterly direction with the stream on your left. The path is indistinct to start with but becomes easier to follow as you descend. As you continue, the path leads you down the mountain into woodland where it becomes a rough stone track between narrow stone walls. Near the bottom there is a wooden gate leading to Aberglaslyn Hall. Ignore this gate and instead turn left down to a wooden footbridge over the Afon Goch. You may want to stop here for a few moments to enjoy the waterfalls above you.

The footpath now brings you out to the A498 where you turn left and walk 100 m until you reach a junction and a road bridge

Pen-y-Gaer hill fort

over the Afon Glaslyn. Turn right and walk across the bridge. On the far side of the river you leave the road through a gate on your left and along a footpath beside the river. This is the fisherman's walk, and takes you north along the riverbank towards Beddgelert. To start with, the path is rocky and there are handholds in the cliff in places where it is narrow. The river below is fast and turbulent as it goes through the gorge. As you walk up the valley, the river becomes more placid and the path improves. On your right you will pass an old sheep-dipping pen, and the narrow-gauge railway will also be on your right.

The riverside walk continues on the right bank for 1 km until you reach a wooden bridge just beyond the railway bridge over the river. Cross over and continue with the river on your right-hand side. Pass though a pair of gates made to resemble fish, and walk

Gelert's grave

on until you come to a gate, alongside a building, next to the river.

Immediately after this gate, turn left and walk away from the river towards Gelert's grave. The grave is under a tree and just beyond it is a stone wall surrounding a bronze statue of the faithful hound.

From the grave you walk north-east through a gate and turn left to rejoin the riverside walk. This will bring you back into Beddgelert. Walk past the church on your left and, after you go through the metal gate, turn left along the road, past the toilets.

As you continue along the road there is a building with a plaque referring to *The Inn of the Sixth Happiness*. This film, starring Ingrid Bergman, was shot on location around Beddgelert in 1958. The story, about missionary Gladys Aylward, takes place in China, and local mountains were used as the backdrop. The producers even built a mock Chinese town nearby.

When you come to the bridge on your right, ignore it and walk straight on, heading west. This will bring you back to the Royal Goat Hotel and the car park.

Interestingly, the story of Gelert appears to have been created (or perhaps developed) by the manager of the newly opened Beddgelert Hotel in 1803. He enlisted the help of several locals to build the grave and started spreading the legend to encourage people to visit Beddgelert and stay at the hotel. Today the business has been renamed The Royal Goat Hotel.

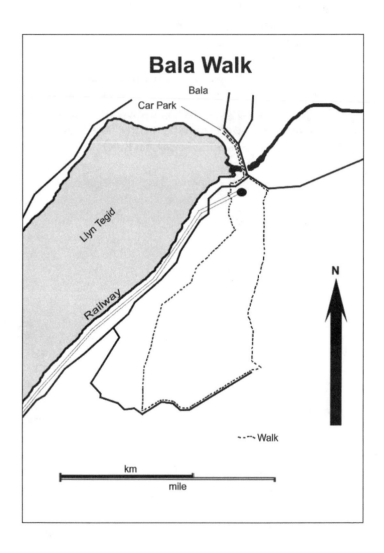

Bala Walk

Bala

Car Park

Llyn Tegid

Railway

N

---- Walk

km

mile

12

Tegid and the Harpist

Tegid Foel (*Tegid the Bald*) was a warrior prince. He lived with his wife, Ceridwen, in a beautiful palace, sheltered in a valley surrounded by mountains. They had two children, a daughter, Creirwy and a son Morfran. Creirwy was beautiful but their son, Morfran, was ugly and dim-witted. His skin was dark, like leather. The people called him Afagddu, which means 'utter darkness'; for his appearance and manners were so repulsive he darkened any room he entered.

Ceridwen, who was a sorceress, loved her children equally and was determined to help her son. She took the ancient cauldron of wisdom and brewed a potion of herbs and poisons so strong that drinking just three drops would give incredible knowledge and intelligence. A blind servant was given the job of stirring the broth and sat labouring beside the roaring fire. As the servant stirred, three drops splashed from the giant pot onto his hand. Without thinking, the servant licked his fingers and in the blink of an eye he became a great bard destined to write fine poetry and sing beautiful songs throughout the land.

Later, when three drops were given to Morfran nothing happened. The magic of the potion was spent and the youth remained hideous and stupid. Ceridwen cleaned out the ancient cauldron and boiled another brew but it made no difference. The ancient cauldron of wisdom had lost its magic.

As the years passed, Tegid watched his son grow more

gruesome and dull. Slowly Tegid's unhappiness festered and his heart turned to anger. He began to hate. He hated his wife for failing to give the boy intelligence. He hated the people who sneered and whispered behind his back. He hated himself for failing to provide a male heir for his lands. Most of all he hated his son, Morfran, for being so ugly and stupid.

As Tegid's hatred grew he became a cruel tyrant. The people began to fear him and hide whenever he rode near. The palace became a place of darkness, filled with loathing and disgust. The bile and spite spread like some dank mist and leached into the ground. The river that once made the valley so fertile drained away, leaving nothing but dust. The valley withered and the crops failed. The people blamed Tegid for the famine and turned against him.

Ceridwen was sad to see such hatred and anger. She knew the valley needed laughter and happiness to thrive. It was time to end the bitterness before it destroyed them all. Ceridwen invited all the villagers to the palace. She ordered food to be fetched from far away. She prepared a great feast and summoned the greatest harpist in the land. Fine food and beautiful music would, she thought, lift the gloom that was suffocating the valley.

The day of the feast arrived. As the people entered the palace the harpist entranced them with gentle melodies that floated through the rooms. As he played a tiny bird flew into the palace, landed on the harp and started to sing. The people ate and drank greedily, glad of the free food and wine. As they drank they became merry. Ceridwen was pleased. Her plan was working.

The harpist continued to fill the air with gentle melodies, but the people had stopped listening to the music. The wine they had drunk so greedily dulled their senses and made them aggressive. They scorned and sneered at the prince and his ugly son and laughed with contempt as they filled their goblets from the great

Llyn Tegid, the largest natural lake in Wales

vats. The feast became a drunken frenzy and the palace was filled with spite and venom. Tegid leapt up and shouted at his guests, ordering them to leave, but it made no difference.

The harpist stopped playing and heard a shrill voice. It was the little bird. It cried, '*Der, der. Dial a ddaw. Dial a ddaw*' (Come away. Come away. Vengeance has come. Vengeance has come').

The harpist wondered what the little bird meant.

'*Der, der. Dial a ddaw. Dial a ddaw*', cried the little bird for a second time, and fluttered up onto the man's sleeve.

The tiny bird pulled at the cloth tugging with his beak until the musician stood up. The little bird continued to pull and the harpist found himself being led from the palace, in such haste that he left his harp behind. No one noticed him leaving. The man, led by the little bird, climbed up away from the palace, leaving the noise of the revellers far below. Just as they reached the top of the mountain there was a giant crashing sound. Water thundered across the land. The harpist looked back. A vast river was surging across the valley, destroying everything in its path.

The harpist sat on the mountain watching, horrified, as farms and villages were washed away. By the morning the thunder of water had gone. A great lake had appeared, filling the valley from end to end and drowning the evil prince and his spiteful people.

The little bird's warning had been true. Vengeance had come. The man searched for the little bird that had saved him, but it was gone. Slowly the harpist climbed back down the mountain. The surface of the lake lay still as glass, the silent water hiding its terrible secret. The man, now alone, stood on the bank. A strange gurgling sound erupted from deep within the lake. Something emerged from the gloomy depths and bubbled to the surface. It was a harp.

Today Llyn Tegid, as it is known, hides the secret of the drowned palace 150 feet beneath its waves, while the teachers of Bala proudly tutor their scholars in the beauty and magic of Celtic harp music.

Bala Walk

Llyn Tegid near Bala, at a length of 4½ miles, is the largest natural lake in Wales. Originally created by glacial erosion, the cold waters of Llyn Tegid contain a strange fish, the 'Gwyniad', that is unique to the lake. Bala, the town at the northern end of the lake, was created by Royal Charter in 1310 and has a charming main street with a variety of shops, restaurants and public houses. The walk starts from a small car park near the lake and travels uphill, south of the town, giving magnificent views of the lake and surrounding mountains, before returning to Bala past the narrow gauge railway that runs along the southern shore of the lake. Bala is located on the A494, 17 miles north-east of Dolgellau and 18 miles west of Llangollen. The free car park is on the B4391 between the lake shore and Heol Tegid (Tegid Road).

Ordnance Survey map number 125 grid reference SH 928 353
Latitude = 52.9058, Longitude = -3.5951
Lat = 52 degrees, 54.3 minutes North
Long = 3 degrees, 35.7 minutes West

Length	5.34 km – 3.32 miles
Maximum height	330.73 m
Minimum height	158.59 m
Height ascended	208.13 m
Navigation	Easy
Difficulty	Moderate
Estimated time	2 hours 16 minutes

Leave the car park and walk south along the footpath beside the lake so that the lake is on your right. The path will take you over a road bridge crossing the Dee. After 350 m you will come to a road junction. Alongside the junction is a stone bridge that is for pedestrian use only. Continue along the road taking the left fork. Walk a further 200 m, passing a road-salt depot on your left, until you reach a bridleway on your right, which you take.

Continue along the bridleway for 120 m, where the footpath you want leaves to the left and you climb up through woodland, walking south, for 500 m until you arrive at a stile. Cross the stile and emerge from the wood, continuing to walk uphill and following the left-hand fence line. This will bring you to the next stile, at the top of the field. From here there are panoramic views of Llyn Tegid, Bala and the mountains beyond.

This stile leads to the next field, which you cross diagonally to another stile and the next field where you follow the right-hand fence. When you reach a ladder stile climb over and walk up the bank, following the footpath south across open scrubland. After the next ladder stile you reach a house and a single-track road where you turn right and continue south-west along the road. To start with the road is level. It then climbs, turns west and start to descend taking you through a gate and over a cattle grid.

Shortly after the cattle grid a footpath leaves the road to the right, which you follow so that you are walking north back towards Llyn Tegid. From this vantage point you have clear views of the entire length of the lake. The footpath now meanders downhill across open scrub to a stile where it continues with a low stone wall on your left. The path continues around the small cottage and up a bank before resuming its descent towards Bala. As you descend you pass a larger house on your left and arrive at a stile leading to the manicured grounds of the Bala Lake Hotel. Cross the stile and take the path just below and to the left of the wooden forest gate. The footpath passes just in front of the hotel where it joins a lane travelling north-east.

Walk along the lane for 400 m, passing a house on your left, until you reach a gate and stile. Cross the stile and walk across the field following the left-hand fence to a ladder stile leading to the next field. Walk north across this field aiming for a house and metal bridge on the far side. Cross the stile in front of the bridge and walk across the bridge over the railway line to the platform. You are now in the station, which is the end of the line for the Bala Lake Railway. Originally owned by Great Western Railways, this was part of the Ruabon to Barmouth line and it operated using standard-gauge track, which has long since gone. It reopened as a narrow-gauge railway in 1972, with services between Bala, Llanuwchllyn and Llangower during the summer, using steam and diesel engines.

Leave the station using the entrance and the metal stile leading to the road, which you cross. Walk over the pedestrian stone bridge you passed at the start of the walk. From here you return along the edge of the lake and over the Dee back to the car park.

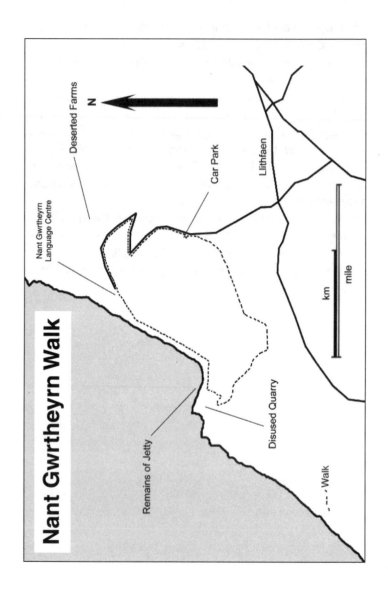

Nant Gwrtheyrn Walk

N

Deserted Farms

Nant Gwrtheyrn
Language Centre

Car Park

Llithfaen

Remains of Jetty

Disused Quarry

km

mile

- - - Walk

13

The Curse of Nant Gwrtheyrn

Gwrtheyrn was a Brythonic King who lived in Kent during the fifth century. He was a timid man and his kingdom was weak. He employed mercenaries from Saxony to fight his enemies and paid them with gold. The Saxons, led by the brutal warrior Hengist, drove off Gwrtheyrn's foes. King Gwrtheyrn was pleased and gave Hengist the Isle of Thanet as a reward. The Saxons bought their families to Kent and settled on the fertile island. Before long, they started to take more land. Seeing the danger he had invited into his kingdom, Gwrtheyrn negotiated a wedding to protect his throne. He asked for the hand of Alys, the beautiful daughter of Hengist, the Saxon leader. Hengist agreed to the match, and a great feast was prepared, with Saxons and Britons sitting together. Suddenly, as one, the Saxons jumped up, drew their daggers and stabbed the Britons beside them. Gwrtheyrn had been tricked. He escaped and ran for his life, accompanied by druid priests.

The king and his priests travelled far across the land looking for a remote part of Britain where the evil Hengist would never find them. After years of searching, they found a small valley, hidden behind a mountain, on a remote peninsula. The land could be ploughed and there were fish in the sea. King Gwrtheyrn had found his refuge and the little party settled in the valley. They built houses and soon a thriving village was established, a village that was so remote that it should never be discovered.

One hundred years later, three Christian monks found a tiny

track leading down a steep mountain and followed it to the valley below. Near the sea, they found a village with a pagan temple. The monks told the villagers to build a Christian church, but the people refused. They threw stones at the monks and drove them away. The retreating monks stopped on the track, high above the village, and each monk cursed the tiny hamlet below them.

'The ground in this valley is unholy. No man shall be buried here,' yelled the first monk.

'The men of Nant Gwrtheyrn shall never marry the women of Nant Gwrtheyrn,' cried the second monk.

'Your village is doomed and will be ruined three times. The third time it falls it will be for ever,' bellowed the third monk.

The people in the valley heard the curses and laughed at the monks. 'Words cannot hurt us,' they said.

The following day the men of the village took their boats into the bay to fish. A violent storm blew up and overturned the boats, drowning the men. The bodies disappeared into the sea. With no men, the women had no choice but to leave the village and start new lives. Nant Gwrtheyrn became a deserted ruin.

As the years passed people began to return to the valley to farm, but strange accidents happened to the men. Some fell into the sea and disappeared beneath the waves. Others vanished into the forest, never to be seen again. Slowly the graveyard filled up with headstones carved with the names of their widows. Wary of the curses, the people dared not wed each other. The men travelled away from the village to find their wives and bring them back to the valley. Small farms were started but they were so far from any market and the track out of the valley was so steep that the farmers struggled to make a living.

Eventually people gave up and drifted away until there were only three farms left at Nant Gwrtheyrn called Tŷ Hen, Tŷ Canol and Tŷ Uchaf.

An abandoned farmhouse, one of several near the village

At Tŷ Uchaf lived Rhys Maredydd with his sister Angharad. They were orphans. Their father had been consumed in a terrible fire that had destroyed the winter hay. Their mother had died of a broken heart. The orphans had a cousin, Meinir who lived with her father at Tŷ Hen. The three children were friends and would play together when their jobs were done.

As the youngsters grew older, Rhys and his cousin Meinir fell in love. They wandered hand in hand on Yr Eifl, the mountain above the farms. A great oak tree stood on the mountain where they would sit and plan their lives together, sheltered by the giant branches. When Rhys asked Meinir for her hand in marriage she willingly agreed, and the happy couple ran down the mountain to seek her father's permission.

'You cannot marry Rhys,' said her father.
'But we love each other,' cried Meinir.

'Rhys is your cousin. You cannot marry your neighbour. Remember the curse,' said her father.

Tears ran down Meinir's face as her father spoke and his heart melted. He relented and embraced the young lovers, agreeing they could wed. Plans were made for the wedding. It was agreed they would wed far away from Nant Gwrtheyrn, at the church of Clynnog Fawr. Surely the curse would not hurt them there.

The morning of the wedding arrived. It was a fine summer's day. Rhys dressed in his Sunday clothes and walked across the fields to Meinir's farm. Her father stood in the doorway solemnly refusing entry, as was the custom. Eventually, to the merriment of the gathering wedding guests, Meinir's father grinned and stood aside. Rhys went inside to find his bride. Searching for the bride on the wedding morning is another ancient custom and Rhys went from room to room happily calling for Meinir to reveal herself, but she did not appear. Meinir, eager to make Rhys work to find her, had slipped away to hide, long before her betrothed had arrived.

Enjoying the game, Rhys searched the barn and the cowsheds, but they were empty. Meinir had vanished. He called her name, but there was no answer. The wedding guests cheered and encouraged Rhys as he went from field to field looking for his bride. The morning passed and the sun beat down. Rhys grew hot in his wedding suit. He was no longer enjoying searching for Meinir. He called again. Still there was no answer.

'Perhaps she has gone to Clynnog Fawr and is waiting for you at the church,' said the wedding guests.

Rhys set off along the track, leading up the mountain towards Clynnog Fawr. The wedding guests followed behind as quickly as they could. But Meinir was not waiting at the church. Rhys turned and ran back towards Nant Gwrtheyrn, desperate to find his bride. Meinir's father, weary from the long walk to the church, borrowed a horse and galloped after Rhys.

The two men searched the farm again but could not find Meinir. The dark came but they did not stop. They cut torches and scoured the mountain through the night, calling for Meinir to reveal herself ...

Rhys and Meinir's father continued to search as the months passed. Then one night Meinir's father did not return from the search. He was never seen again. Rhys was alone in the valley.

The corn went uncut and the cows grew wild as Rhys searched. Summer turned to winter but he would not stop. Each day Rhys would walk for miles called out, 'Meinir, Meinir, where are you?'

Each night he would sit huddled under the great oak tree on the mountain and cry softly, 'Meinir, Meinir, where are you?'

Thirty years passed, then one night as Rhys sat shivering under the great tree, storm clouds gathered on the mountain. A flash of lightning struck the tree, splitting it in two. A hideous cry echoed across the valley for, in the flash of light, Meinir's hiding place had been revealed. There, wedged in the hollow trunk of the tree, stood the twisted skeleton of a young woman. All that was left of the wedding dress, once so pure and white, were a few grey rags hanging from the bones.

Rhys was found next morning lying dead beneath the tree, with Meinir's corpse in his arms.

The curse of Nant Gwrtheyrn had left the valley desolate and empty for the second time.

It would be another 200 years before Nant Gwrtheyrn became ruined for the third and final time ...

Nant Gwrtheyrn Walk

The village of Nant Gwrtheyrn had lain empty for many years, a derelict ruin, and a victim of either the curse or economic reality when the granite quarries were abandoned. Pictures taken in the 1970s show the place neglected and deserted. More recently the village has been taken over and redeveloped with funding from the National Lottery. Residential courses are held here for people of all levels to learn Welsh as a second language. The centre also hosts weddings in its chapel, and the cottages are available for holidays aside from the language courses.

In his book *The Lost Villages of Britain* Richard Muir describes Nant Gwrtheyrrn as 'A place glorious in its beauty with the ideal qualities combined to produce perfection'.

Nant Gwrtheyrn is not shown on most maps. To reach the village, head for the nearby village of Llithfaen, which is 6 miles north of Pwllheli on the B4417 and 15 miles west of Porthmadog. Once you are in Llithfaen follow the signpost for Nant Gwrtheyrn, pointing along a small road going north.

Our walk starts in the top car park, high above the village. It

Ordnance Survey map number 123 grid reference SH 353 439
Latitude = 52.9686, Longitude = -4.4538
Lat = 52 degrees, 58.1 minutes North
Long = 4 degrees, 27.2 minutes West

Length	5.68 km – 3.52 miles
Maximum height	277.54 m
Minimum height	7.82 m
Height ascended	357.84 m
Navigation	Easy
Difficulty	Moderate
Estimated time	2 hours 56 minutes

Nant Gwrtheyrn today, refurbished and thriving
as a language and cultural centre

takes you steeply down through a conifer forest with views of the sea and the old workings, and the decaying farmhouses in the valley below, and eventually into the village at the base of the mountain Yr Eifl. There is a café with toilets in the village. From there you walk along the shingle beach to the old quarry at Penrhyn Glas and climb back to high ground, before returning across farmland with fine view to the north and south of the Llŷn peninsula.

The first point of interest is in the top car park, where you will see a sculpture containing three standing stones, erected to celebrate the work of the quarrymen of Nant Gwrtheyrn. Leave the car park, continuing along the road you have just arrived by so that you are walking north-east. The road goes downhill and as it does so turns so that you are walking north-west. After 500 m the road turns sharp right and continues steeply downhill. If you look down you will see a line of cottages laid out in the valley. This is Nant Gwrtheyrn. Deserted farmhouses and outbuildings litter the valley floor and high on the mountains opposite there is evidence of the quarries that used to support the village.

The road continues steeply downhill as you walk east for the next 400 m, where it turns north-west and leads down to the village. This is a new road. The old track it replaced was much steeper, with a gradient of up to 33 per cent or 1 in 3! – it can still be seen coming down through the trees. The road down and the surrounding mountains have a pleasant continental feel about them, with the smell of fresh pine and stunning views. As you enter the village go over the cattle grid and bear left. This will take you past the chapel on your left, which is now a heritage centre.

The village's two rows of houses are known as Trem y Môr (sea view) and Trem y Mynydd (mountain view). The houses were built in 1878 to house workers in the recently-opened granite quarries. A pier was built from the beach and pre-cut granite pieces, known as setts, were loaded onto steamers for shipping to England, and used for paving the burgeoning cities of Lancashire. The village went into terminal decline during World War II when the population abandoned the place. Was it the third and final destruction as foretold by the monks?

Happily, that is not the end of the story. The curse was finally broken when, in 1978, the derelict village was purchased from Amey Roadstone for £25,000 and renovation began to create a residential Welsh-language centre.

Just past the chapel you reach the café, where it is possible to sit outside and enjoy the views of the sea and take refreshments. From the café you continue towards the beach along the path, aiming for the disused quarry south-west along the coast. After 100 m the path forks and you bear left towards the sea and

Nant Gwrtheyrn beach, looking north from the disused quarry

The same beach but looking south towards the disused quarry;
the jetty was just below the quarry

redundant buildings on the shoreline. When you reach a post with a 'Llŷn Coastal Path' marker, walk down to the beach and turn left along the shingle.

As you walk towards the beach you may notice the ground is grey ash and cinders. This is residue from the steam boilers that drove the engines moving the limestone in the quarries. Signs of cable systems can be seen in the old buildings nearby and on the mountain high above the village behind you.

Porth-y-nant beach is made of shingle that the tides have arranged in steps. As you walk along the beach you pass rusty pieces of ironwork standing proud like strange art forms in nature's gallery, more evidence of the long-gone workers who lived at Nant Gwrtheyrn.

After 800 m the beach curves so that you are walking west, and another 270 m brings you to Penrhyn Glas. From the top of the beach leave along the path that starts climbing, going over a small bridge across a stream, and then again climbs for a few metres where you turn left up steps, marked by a post with a blue band.

As you climb, the path takes you back across the stream and then climbs south-west to the top of the cliff where it meets a grass track. Turn right along the track and cross the stream, following the track west for a short distance until it turns left away from the sea. Continue along the track, over a cattle grid and uphill in a south-east direction. After 600 m you reach a T-junction. Go across the junction in the tracks and over the stile opposite, following the footpath that climbs up and to the east.

From here the footpath climbs steeply for 200 m taking you past a metal ladder stile on your right and bringing you to a wooden gate in a stone wall. Go through the gate, into the next field and walk north-east for 180 m to a metal gate leading to another field. Continue north-east across the field to a post with a red band at the top of the field. From here you have panoramic views, looking north to Caernarfon Bay and Anglesey, and south-east to Cardigan Bay and Barmouth.

Keep walking north-east, aiming for the highest point ahead of you until you reach a stone wall and metal gate to your right. Go through the gate into the next field and continue north-east, keeping next to the stone wall on your left, until you reach the next gate and another field. Continue walking along the left-hand side of the field as it bends slowly left. After 420 m you arrive at a metal gate leading to a path. Walk 100 m along the path to the road and turn left to walk for a short distance back to the car park.

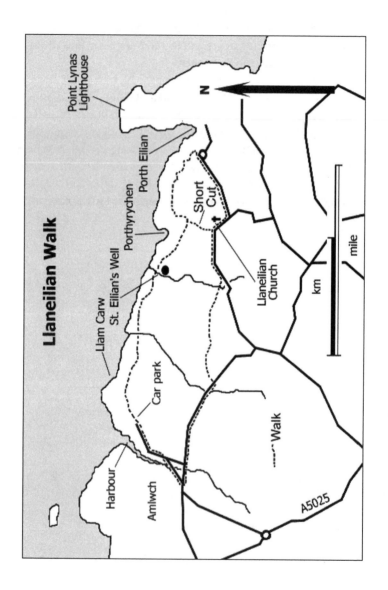

Llaneilian Walk

Point Lynas Lighthouse
Porth Eilian
Porthyrychen
Llam Carw
St. Eilian's Well
Short Cut
Llaneilian Church
N
km
mile
Car park
Walk
Harbour
Amlwch
A5025

14

St Eilian and the Leaping Deer

In the fifth century, following St Patrick's success in Ireland, the Pope sent many good, pious men on missions to spread the word of God in Britain. One such man was St Eilian. He sailed from Rome, with his family, in a small boat loaded with all his worldly possessions. Unsure of the nature of Britain and determined to be self-sufficient, Eilian included cattle, sheep and a deer in his cargo.

Eilian was a quiet, confident man, slow to anger but single-minded in his task. He had a way with animals. They responded well to his soothing words and the animals became pets during the long voyage. The deer, a handsome stag, was his favourite.

After many weeks at sea, Eilian landed at a small inlet called Porth-yr-ychen on the island of Anglesey and began to unload. The ruler of the Island was Cadwallon Law Hir (*Cadwallon Long Hand*), prince of Gwynedd. Word reached him that a strange foreigner had arrived. The prince sent his men to investigate. Cadwallon's men hid on the cliff and watched as the animals waded ashore and began to climb up from the beach. They were fine-looking beasts. Eager to please their master, the men decided to ambush Eilian and steal his cows. They knew that Cadwallon would value such prize animals.

Cadwallon's men arranged themselves on each side of the path hidden in the bracken. After a short time Eilian passed them, followed by his cattle and sheep. The deer, sensing that something was wrong, hung back from the rest of the animals, pawing the ground. The robbers ran from their cover, knocked Eilian to the ground and with loud yells drove the animals away.

That night, one of Eilian's cows was slowly roasted over a fire pit at Cadwallon's castle as the men celebrated with their master. Later in the evening, when their bellies were full of meat and wine, there was a loud bang on the outer gate. The guard peered over the battlements and did not believe what he saw. Outside the castle was a large stag, and on its back sat a man.

'Who are you and what is your business at this hour?' demanded the guard.

'I am Eilian and I have come for my animals,' replied the man on the stag.

The guard ran to the great hall to tell his prince of the strange caller. Cadwallon laughed when he heard the news. 'Fetch him in, stag and all,' he bellowed.

Solemnly Eilian, still astride the stag, was led into the hall. Cadwallon studied his visitor while his men sat silently waiting for a command from their prince. Menace filled the air.

'What can we do for you, Eilian?' asked Cadwallon, smirking at his guest.

'You, my lord, have something that belongs to me,' said Eilian firmly.

'And what might that be?' replied the Prince.

'My sheep and cattle. I want them back,' said Eilian.

'Eilian wants his sheep and cattle back,' scoffed Cadwallon to his men. They laughed.

'Do you own any land?' asked Cadwallon, turning back to Eilian.

'I do not,' replied Eilian.

'I see that you are a foreigner, so you have no right to graze on common land,' said the prince, adding 'but I am a fair man. When I see that you own some land you can have your animals. Until

148

St Eilian's church

then I will keep them safe here, with my stock.'

'You see nothing but your own greed,' answered Eilian. He turned his mount and the stag walked out of the great hall.

That night, as he slept, Cadwallon went blind.

Eilian returned to Porth-yr-ychen and started to build a church, just to the west of the inlet, beside a small stream. He added a well beside his church and, before long, people began to visit him, to listen to his teachings and to drink the pure water from his well. The water from the well had mysterious powers, curing the sick and, some said, restoring sight. Stories spread far and wide telling the tale of St Eilian's sacred well.

Cadwallon, the blind prince, knew that he had been wrong to steal Eilian's cattle. His heart was full of remorse. He ordered that all of Eilian's stock should be returned to Eilian and sent the animals back to their rightful owner with a message of repentance and humility. Eilian replied, asking the prince to visit him without delay. Cadwallon was led on his horse to the holy man's little church.

Seeing Cadwallon's humility and sorrow Elian forgave him. Eilian bathed his eyes and the prince's sight was restored.

'How may I repay you?' asked the prince.

'Let me have enough land to keep my animals on. That is all I ask,' replied the holy man.

'How much do you want?' asked Cadwallon, feeling far less humble now that his sight was restored.

'Let us settle the amount with a race,' answered Eilian.

'What sort of race?' asked the prince.

'Your hunting dogs shall chase my stag starting from here. The place where they catch him will be the boundary of the land you shall grant me,' replied Eilian.

Cadwallon liked the idea. He owned the fastest hunting dogs in the land. They would soon catch the stag, he thought. He agreed and the race began.

Eilian's stag ran like the wind, but the dogs strained to keep up. The stag thundered across the countryside with the dogs close behind. It was going to be a short race. Then the stag leapt a huge gorge and disappeared into the distance. The dogs, unable to cross the chasm, returned dejected to their master.

The gorge the stag leapt is known today as Llam y Carw (the stag's leap). Prince Cadwallon kept his word, and that is how St Eilian became one of the most powerful and biggest landowners on Anglesey.

A religious community grew at Llaneilian and for centuries the sacred stream served the holy order well. Pilgrims travelled for miles to pay a groat, a silver coin worth two pence, for the healing water, and Llaneilian grew into one of the richest churches in Wales.

Llaneilian Walk

The walk to Llaneilian begins at Amlwch Port, with a walk along the cliff top coastal path to Porth Eilian, where it turns and returns inland through the village of Llaneilian and back to Amlwch. The huge copper mine that was Parys Mountain is to the south of the town, and Amlwch Port was the point of export of this highly prized metal in the days of sail, when the harbour buzzed with activity. This is an easy, scenic walk along the cliffs and includes Llaneilian church, the home of notable medieval painted panels. Because of the importance of its contents, the church is normally locked. Amlwch is located on the A5025, 15 miles north-west of the Menai Bridge. As you arrive at Amlwch, turn right at the first roundabout and head for Amlwch Port. The free car park is just east of the harbour at the top of Upper Quay Street. There are public toilets at Amlwch Port and near the beach at Porth Eilian.

Ordnance Survey map number 114 grid reference SH 452 935
Latitude = 53.4161, Longitude = -4.3292
Lat = 53 degrees, 25.0 minutes North
Long = 4 degrees, 19.8 minutes West

Length	6.28 km – 3.90 miles
Maximum height	40.46 m
Minimum height	1.99 m
Height ascended	153.64 m
Navigation	Easy
Difficulty	Easy
Estimated time	2 hours 27 minutes

Begin the walk by leaving the car park, travelling past a notice board and heading north-east. Aim for a house further along the cliff. The footpath continues to the right of the house where there is a gate, which you go through. Shortly after the house the path turns south-east and takes you around the top of Llam Carw (the stag's leap) where St Eilian's stag escaped from the hounds by jumping across the gorge.

200 m further on you come to a fork in the path. Take the left-hand path, following the yellow arrows. After a short distance you reach a wooden bridge, a kissing gate and a sign indicating that you are walking the Copper Coastal Trail. In the distance you will see Point Lynas, used by pilots waiting to join vessels returning to Liverpool. The first lighthouse, established in 1779, was simply a farmhouse with oil lamps hung on a tower. The new lighthouse was built in 1835 at a cost of £1165.

Continue along the coastal path for 500 m, when you will reach a kissing gate and another wooden bridge. This is the bridge over the stream that is Ffynnon Eilian (Eilian's well). The well and the remains of a small chapel are to the right of the footpath, just after the stream.

Although the well was considered to have healing powers, it also had a more sinister use and was used to curse people. As late as the eighteenth century, the well was considered powerful enough to cripple and even kill the intended victims. In 1925 a wax effigy was found in the well, pinned to a piece of slate. The slate had the initials RF scratched on it and the effigy's head, legs and one arm had been snapped off. Clearly someone did not like RF and wished them harm.

Continue through the next kissing gate and walk south-east for 250 m where you reach a series of six steps and a gate taking you over an outcrop of rock. Continue for another 200 m where you will reach two kissing gates with a short climb between them. Between the gates there is a footpath leading to the right, heading inland. Our journey continues straight on through the

The clifftop path heads towards Point Lynas in the distance

second gate, but if you want to shorten the walk it is possible to turn right and take a short cut up the hill to Llaneilian. This will reduce the length of the walk by about 1.5 km. Below you on your left is the cove Porth-y-rychen, where St Eilian landed with his animals.

From the second kissing gate turn left, heading north-east, and aiming for Point Lynas. The footpath crosses a field and then turns south-east before it meanders down the cliff to the beach at Porth Eilian. As you descend into the shelter of the bay the vegetation becomes more succulent, changing from heathers and gorse to wild fuchsias and dog roses.

When you reach the beach, walk south-west along the road that goes uphill for 700 m. There are toilets a short distance up the hill on the left. At the top of the hill you will have a view of Mynydd Eilian to the south. The hill was used during the

Napoleonic wars for a lookout point and signal station to warn of any French attack.

At the end of the road there is a T-junction where you turn right and walk for another 200 m. This will bring you to Llaneilian where the church is on your right. If you have taken the shortcut you will have emerged just to the left of the gate leading into the graveyard.

Leave the church and walk west along the lane. The scarred remains of Parys Mountain and the copper workings will be ahead slightly to your left. After 400 m you will reach Bryn Rodyn Cottage on the right. Immediately after the cottage there is a kissing gate where the footpath continues west for 1 km across scrubland, until you emerge onto a small road. Turn right and follow the road down the hill for 1 km into Porth Amlwch. As you walk down the hill you will pass a sign proclaiming the twinning of Amlwch to Sankwia in the Gambia.

At the bottom of the hill turn right opposite the Liverpool Arms public house, and then bear right along Upper Quay Street, which will take you back to the car park. As you walk towards the car park you may want to explore the harbour on your left and visit the Sail Loft Visitor Centre, where there is a café and an exhibition of local heritage.

St Eilian's chapel, built in the fourteenth century, sits at the back of the church and is reached through a narrow, curved passage

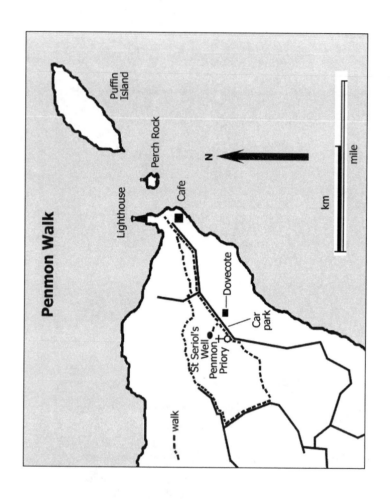

Penmon Walk

Puffin Island

Perch Rock

N

km mile

Lighthouse

Cafe

Dovecote

Car park

St Seriol's Well

Penmon Priory

walk

15

Seiriol the Fair

In 494 AD a baby was born to a royal family. They named him Seiriol. One of his brothers became King Cynlas of Rhos and a second, King Einion of Llŷn, but Seiriol was destined for another life. He chose to go to Anglesey and live as a hermit. Seiriol found a small spring in a cliff near Penmon Point and built a well to catch the water. Beside the well he built a simple stone cell for himself.

News of Seiriol and the pious life he lived spread. People began to journey to Penmon to look at this holy man and to drink the water from his well. Seiriol's holy well, they said, healed the lame and cured the sick. His brothers were concerned for Seiriol and built a priory at Penmon so that he could live in more comfort. Monks came to worship with Seiriol and a community grew up around the holy well. The monks farmed the land and built ponds to provide fresh fish. They lived a frugal life and, with Seiriol's guidance, the priory prospered.

Seiriol yearned for a life of quiet prayer. He needed to get away from Penmon and decided to build a retreat where no one could bother him. He moved to the island half a mile from Penmon where he built a new cell for a bedroom. The island became known as Ynys Seiriol (Seriol's island, also known as *'Puffin Island'*). The Vikings named the island Priestholm because of its religious inhabitant. There was to be no escape for Seiriol, and before long his followers established themselves on the island with their spiritual leader. In 1188 Gerald of Wales recorded 'that the

The dovecote at Penmon, said to be one of the largest in the world

settlement was inhabited by hermits, living by manual labour and serving God.'

No women were allowed on the island and this caused some friction. Sometimes the monks on the island quarrelled, and when they did a plague of rats would appear and devour all their food. Seiriol found the squabbling upsetting. He needed to escape and find somewhere to meditate, away from the island. At low tide there was a small path from the island, which to the mainland and Penmaenmawr, 5 miles across the bay. Seiriol would walk from his island to pray at Penmaenmawr. A chapel was built for him and Seiriol regularly walked across the bay, taking care to return before the incoming tide carried him away.

As Seiriol grew older, he visited other holy men to increase his wisdom and knowledge. He became a friend of St Cybi who lived at Holy Island (*Ynys Gybi*), on the far side of Anglesey. Every morning they both walked 20 miles to meet at the Clorach wells, near Llanerchymedd in the middle of Anglesey, to pray and discuss religious matters. Every evening they both walked 20 miles back to their monasteries. In the mornings Seiriol walked west with the sun at his back, and each evening he walked east, again, with the sun at his back. His face never saw the sun, and his skin was as white as milk. Every morning Cybi walked east with the sun in his face, and each evening he walked west, again, with the sun in his face so that his skin turned as dark as parchment. This is the reason Seiriol is known as Seiriol Wyn (*Seiriol the Fair*) and his friend as Cybi Felyn (*Cybi the Tanned*).

Seiriol retired as abbot and lived to a venerable age. When he died, the monks buried him on his island. Eventually the island was abandoned and Seiriol's remains were removed to Penmon, where he is now buried at the priory. Today, Seiriol's island is also known as Puffin Island.

Penmon Walk

This is a short and relatively easy walk from the priory to the lighthouse at Black Point where you can see Puffin Island and Perch Rock. From there you return in a circular route across farmland and along narrow country lanes to the priory. During the walk you can enjoy views of the Menai approaches, Snowdonia and the north Wales coastline. Penmon priory is located at the eastern end of Anglesey, 5 miles north-east of Beaumaris (*Biwmaris*), and can be reached on the B5109. The Baron Hill Estate owns the land and makes a small charge to park at the priory. Alternatively, drive down to the point where there is a café. Our walk starts at the priory.

Puffin Island is privately owned. Landing on the island is not allowed unless special permission is obtained.

Ordnance Survey map number 115 grid reference 630807
Latitude = 53.3057, Longitude = -4.0562
Lat = 53 degrees, 18.3 minutes North
Long = 4 degrees, 3.4 minutes West

Length	4.76 km – 2.96 miles
Maximum height	79 m
Minimum height	10.9 m
Height ascended	102.6 m
Navigation	Easy
Difficulty	Easy
Estimated time	1 hour 49 minutes

Before you begin your walk, take some time to explore the remains of the priory and the church, where there are ancient Celtic crosses that have been rescued and preserved. One of the

*St Seiriol's well; the cell in which he is reputed
to have lived is on the right*

crosses has had a point sawn off and was being used as a lintel
before being returned to the priory. St Seiriol's remains are under
the altar. At the east end of the car park a gravel path takes you to
St Seiriol's well, and the foundations of the cell where he lived are
nearby.

Opposite the gravel path is a dovecote built in the
seventeenth century to provide fresh meat. Said to contain over
2,000 birds, it is one of the largest of its kind in existence.

You begin the walk by leaving the car park and walking east
along the lane between the well and the dovecote. The lane
continues for just over 1 km until you reach Black Point and the

Puffin Island and Perch Rock, ready to shipwreck unwary sailors

lighthouse. Ahead of you are Puffin Island and Perch Rock, waiting to ensnare passing vessels caught in the racing tides that pass through the narrows.

On the island there is the ruin of a telegraph station, part of the Holyhead to Liverpool system used to alert the Liverpool merchants of the approach of their vessels laden with cargo.

Hunting drastically reduced the island's puffin population, when the birds were pickled in barrels and shipped to France, where they were regarded as a delicacy. Humans also introduced the brown rat, which ate the eggs and drastically reduced puffin numbers. Poisoning of the rats started in 1998 and the puffin population is starting to recover. On your right are the mudflats that St Seiriol walked across at low tide.

From the lighthouse you turn westward and leave the lane and take the footpath opposite the café. You now walk 300 m to a T-junction in the path where you go straight on until you reach a wooden gate. Around 70 m beyond the gate there is a lane where you turn right and follow the lane for 40 m until you reach a kissing gate on your left. The footpath now continues along the right-hand side of a field bordered with sloe bushes. From here you have particularly stunning views of Snowdonia.

The footpath leads to a stone wall with a gate, and from here you walk north-west through a field with a high stone wall on your left. At the next kissing gate the path turns west. Walk for 440 m heading for Pentir, with a white cottage in the distance. At Pentir continue straight on and follow the lane as it zig-zags to a small T-junction at Caim, where you turn left heading south.

Walk along the lane for 500 m until you reach a stone stile on your left with eight steps leading up to a gate. This is where the footpath turns east across open land. Head initially for the redundant lime kiln and quarry on the foreshore and then bear left as the priory comes into view. The quarries here provided the stone for Beaumaris castle. The footpath will bring you back to the road you arrived along by car. Turn left and walk a few more steps back to the priory car park.

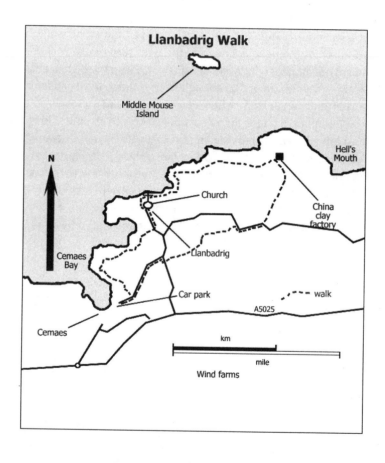

Llanbadrig Walk

Middle Mouse Island

Hell's Mouth

N

Church

China clay factory

Cemaes Bay

Llanbadrig

Car park

walk

A5025

Cemaes

km

mile

Wind farms

16

St Patrick's Shipwreck

In 432 AD an open boat was sailing from England to Ireland when it was caught in a storm. The wind had quickly strengthened from the west during the afternoon. By the evening the little vessel was being driven east, unable to reach a safe haven. The sail had shredded in a violent gust. The crew was wet and cold. They huddled together in the bottom of the boat, exhausted from battling with the wind, helpless and afraid as the stricken craft rolled and pitched through the mountainous waves. They could hear the thunder of water crashing against cliffs somewhere nearby in the darkness.

Only one man showed no fear on that dark night. Bishop Patrick was used to danger. His journey from Rome had been full of adventure. From the beginning, when the Holy Father Pope Celestine had given the Bishop his mission to convert Ireland to the true faith, Patrick had known that it would test his devotion and his courage to the limit.

The journey to Ireland had been a long one. Surely, he thought, God would not bring him so far just to be drowned on the final sea voyage. He knelt and prayed for the vessel to survive the storm. The wind swung to larboard away from the coast and the little vessel turned, towards the open sea, away from the land, away from certain disaster on the jagged cliffs that thundered in the darkness. The Bishop crossed himself and muttered a silent thanks to God for His timely intervention.

There was a flash of lightning. In that second the sailors saw the rocks ahead. The boat, lifted by a giant wave, rose above the rocks and then dropped like a stone. The keel snapped and the vessel disintegrated, throwing men and cargo into the churning water.

By the first light of dawn the wind had died down. Bishop Patrick was lying on the rocks half-submerged in a pool of salty water. He sat up and looked around. He was alone. As the light improved, Patrick found that he was stranded on a small barren island. He was hungry. The salt had split his lips and his throat was swollen. In the distance he could see land.

Patrick searched the island for wreckage, anything that would ease his thirst and hunger. He found a wine bladder caught up in the rocks. It was full. He pulled out the stopper and drank deeply. The wine burned as he swallowed. Nearby was a shattered basket of loaves. Its contents, soaked by the sea, lay ruined on the ground. Patrick ate greedily and drank more wine to mask the salty taste of the bread. Then he prayed and slept.

The sun was high in the sky when he woke. His head ached and he had a foul taste in his mouth. The wine and the salty bread had done their worst. He stood up and looked at the land. Somehow he thought he had to escape from his island prison. An idea came to him.

He poured the last of the wine away and blew into the bladder. When it was inflated he fitted the stopper, pushing it firmly home. He tied the bladder to his body, jumped into the sea and started to swim towards the land. The cold water cleared his head and, to start with, Patrick made good progress. As Patrick swam, the current carried him along the coast towards high cliffs, where there was no chance of getting ashore. He swam until, weary, cold and thirsty, he realised that swimming against the current was hopeless. He floated exhausted, with the bladder resting under his stomach as the tide carried him along. Now the current was carrying him further out to sea.

Patrick mumbled a quiet prayer and sank into a dull torpor. As he did so, the tide turned and he began to drift back along the coast. A shrill cry above Patrick's head woke him with a start. Patrick looked up to see gulls returning to their nests and squabbling as they arrived. He was floating right below the cliffs. In front of him was a small ledge, level with the sea and a cave. Patrick swam to the ledge, pulled himself out of the water and stumbled into the cave. Inside the cave, water trickled from the roof. He tasted the water. It was fresh and pure. Patrick filled the bladder and drank his fill. His prayer had been answered.

Llanbadrig church, with Ynys Badrig (Mouse Island) in the background

Before continuing his journey to Ireland Patrick built a church at the top of the cliff to give thanks to God for saving him when the ship was wrecked on Middle Mouse Island. The Welsh name for the island is Ynys Badrig (*Patrick's island*). Llanbadrig (*St Patrick's church*) is still standing today, 1600 years later.

Pope Celestine I died in 431 AD, before Patrick reached Ireland. Bishop Patrick's mission to Ireland was a success. He arrived in Ireland in 433 AD, one year after being shipwrecked at Mouse Island and, using the shamrock to explain the holy trinity, introduced Christianity to the Irish. He also, it is said, drove every serpent from the country.

Although Patrick has never been canonised by a pope, he is recognised as a saint by many religious orthodoxies and is the Patron Saint of Ireland, his Saint's Day being celebrated on 17 March each year. Before he died in 493 AD, Patrick wrote his '*Confessio*' (or 'declaration') containing an account of his life.

Llanbadrig Walk

This part of the north coast of Anglesey is an area of outstanding natural beauty, some of which is owned by the National Trust. The Llanbadrig walk is circular and includes a sandy beach, farmland, a derelict china clay factory and a cliff walk. During the walk there are views of Ynys Badrig (*Middle Mouse*), the island where St Patrick was shipwrecked, and a visit to Llanbadrig church, built by St Patrick to give thanks for his survival.

Technologies to generate electricity are evident, including Wylfa nuclear power station to the west, and giant wind farms to the south, each testimony to man's ingenuity or folly. The walk starts from a free car park at the east end of the beach in Cemaes Bay. To reach the car park, turn off the A5025 just east of Cemaes. The turning is signposted to Llanbadrig church. After 600 m you will come to a T-junction where you turn left and drive west for 500 m until you reach the car park. There is a small harbour and toilets just along the promenade towards Cemaes.

Ordnance Survey map number 115 grid reference SH 375 938
Latitude = 53.4153, Longitude = -4.4467
Lat = 53 degrees, 24.9 minutes North
Long = 4 degrees, 26.8 minutes West

Length	5.46 km – 3.39 miles
Maximum height	38.48 m
Minimum height	2.3 m
Height ascended	168.82 m
Navigation	Easy
Difficulty	Moderate
Estimated time	2 hours 22 minutes

Leave the car park and walk east along the lane by which you arrived. After 500 m, when you come to the T-junction, turn right and after 40 m you reach the start of the footpath on your left. Follow the footpath a short distance through woodland to a stile. From the stile, walk another 50 m to a gate. Do not go through the gate. At this point the footpath moves to the right of the gate and continues east with a fence on your left. The path is narrow and can be rather overgrown with bracken in summer.

Walk for another 240 m and you will reach a metal kissing gate. Go through the gate and bear left so that you are walking north-east, across a small field for 70 m, to a stile, which you climb across. The footpath now continues east over a well-manicured lawn to a drive leading to a house on your right. Cross the drive and go over a stile into a field where you continue walking 400 m east. Aim for a stile on the far side of the field.

Cross the stile and turn right along a lane, which you follow for 300 m until the lane turns right. On the left-hand side of the corner there is an opening in the hedge where the footpath leaves the lane and continues north-east. The gap in the hedge is small and it is easy to miss the opening. Go through the gate beyond the hedge and walk north-east across the field keeping to the left-hand side.

After a short distance you join a small track that descends with a large farmhouse on your left. Ignore the turning to the farmhouse and continue north-east as the track heads downhill. At the bottom of the hill you reach a small causeway across reed beds, which you walk over. The reed beds are the scars left from mining china clay from the valley.

At the far end of the causeway, turn left and follow the track taking you to the derelict buildings you will have seen as you walked down the hill earlier. This is the china clay factory at Porth Llanlleiana. The chimney was built further up the cliff to increase

The china clay factory at Porth Llanlleiana;
note that the chimney is further up the hill

its height and improve the draught, helping to fire the kilns. The factory closed in 1920 after being damaged by fire. The pebble beach at Porth Llanlleiana is secluded and a good point to stop for refreshments. From the beach at Porth Llanlleiana you get your first view of Ynys Badrig where St Patrick was shipwrecked in 440 AD. The island is 1 km offshore and the tides here are fierce. St Patrick must have been a very strong swimmer.

Leaving Porth Llanlleiana you join the Anglesey coastal path and walk west. The path starts with twenty-eight concrete steps to a gate where it continues to climb to the top of the cliff. Follow the cliff-top path for 500 m to a set of steps between two gates.

From the second gate you will see Wylfa nuclear power station to the west and the regimented ranks of wind turbines to your south. Further to the west stands the Skerries lighthouse. With good visibility it is possible to see the Mountains of Mourne in Northern Ireland, the Lake District, and the Isle of Man.

Continue walking along the cliff path for another 1 km until you reach the graveyard of Llanbadrig church. Below you at the bottom of the cliff is Ogof Badrig (*St Patrick's cave*) where he sheltered and found fresh water after his desperate swim. The graveyard is enclosed with a low stone wall, and there are ancient stone steps protruding, used in the past to climb over the wall. If you look at Middle Mouse Island from the church it looks more like a giant whale resting on the surface of the sea than a mouse.

The church is worth exploring. Established in 440 AD, it is a modest building. Originally wooden, it was rebuilt in stone and improved over the centuries. The east wall of the graveyard includes an arch that has been blocked up. This was the entrance used by the nuns from an adjacent convent, long since gone, when they visited the church to pray.

In the nineteenth century Lord Henry Stanley, the 3rd Lord Stanley of Alderley restored the church. He had been a diplomat, married a Spanish lady, and adopted many Muslim customs. The blue tiles that surround the altar and the colours of the stained glass windows reflect this influence. When Lord Stanley died in 1903 he left some strange instructions for his burial. He believed that followers of Islam were buried in an upright standing position, facing Mecca, and this is how he was interred.

The pews towards the altar show signs of fire damage caused by vandals in the 1980s when they built a fire in the porch. Following the fire the church was repaired and the pews at the back are new. Gravestones found at Llanbadrig, similar to those found in Rome and dated to the third century, support the connection with St Patrick and his papal mission.

Llanbadrig was used as a location for the 2006 film *Half Light*, starring Demi Moore. To make the church look more authentic the film crew added a cardboard Celtic cross to the apex of the roof.

Leave Llanbadrig church walking south along the lane for 400 m where there is a kissing gate on the right. Go though the gate and walk 100 m where you rejoin the coastal path turning left. The path now follows the cliff south-west for 800 m before turning south-east, and a further 500 m bringing you back to the car park at Cemaes Bay.

Also in this series:

Walking with Welsh Legends
South-western Wales

and coming shortly:

Walking with Welsh Legends
Central Wales

On-line Shop

Our whole catalogue of titles are
available on our website

• Walking and Mountaineering
• Regions of Wales / Local Guides
• Maritime Wales
•Welsh Heritage and Culture
• Art and Photography
• Welsh History and Myths
• Children's Books
✳ Many discounted books ✳

www.carreg-gwalch.com